I'VE BEEN MARCHING ALL THE TIME

AN AUTOBIOGRAPHY

XERNONA CLAYTON

with

HAL GULLIVER

LONGSTREET PRESS
Atlanta, Georgia

Published by
LONGSTREET PRESS, INC.
2150 Newmarket Parkway
Suite 102
Marietta, Georgia 30067

Printed in the United States of America

1st printing 1991

Library of Congress Catalog Card Number 90-063902

ISBN 0-929264-87-8

This book was printed by R. R. Donnelley & Sons, Harrisonburg,
Virginia. The text was set in Sabon by Typo-Repro Service, Inc.,
Atlanta, Georgia.
Book design by Jill Dible.

Dedicated to

*Sharon, Gregory, Bradford, Laura,
Paul, Jr., and John Miles*

*in hopes that they will
march down the road in
quest for a better world*

ACKNOWLEDGMENTS

There can be no full accounting of my debt to the hundreds of people who have made a difference in my life and as a result have contributed, in one way or another, to the shaping of this book.

To my parents who gave love, guidance, and laughter all in proper order . . . to my sister Xenobia, brother James, and nieces and nephews who help me remember my childhood with such fond memories . . . to all of my teachers (in school and in church) and the neighborhood people who cared . . . and to my friends, too many to name, I say thanks.

The countless friends who have been supportive beyond description include: Coretta Scott King, Lillian Miles Lewis, Jo Bridges, Linda Hollingsworth Johnson, Dorothye Boswell, Dorothea Foster, and Earlene Harris.

I am grateful to those very busy people who took time from their demanding schedules to read the manuscript and provide generous comments on the book. I am also grateful to my husband, Paul, who read the manuscript and offered many suggestions and valuable perceptions.

Paul's family has been a significant source of inspiration to me, including his mother, Jessie, Aunt Cindy and Uncle Alvin, other uncles and aunts, and his enormous clan of wonderful cousins. I have a special admiration for his brothers and sisters — Lindell, Arthur, Mary, and Wilma — and their spouses — Peggy, Clay, and Henry. I have also received great encouragement from my sister-in-law Thelma and brother-in-law Tony.

A very special thank-you to my administrative assistant, Gioconda Miller, who spent her evenings and weekends researching, verifying, and doing necessary follow-up to ensure clarity and accuracy. Her dedication and willingness to do whatever it takes has been a tremendous source of support. Thanks go also to Erica Weaver, who transcribed the tapes for editing.

I am indebted to those entities who have provided me a fulfilling and challenging professional career — mayors, governors, the SCLC, American Friends Service Committee, WAGA-TV, and Turner Broadcasting.

I consider it a high privilege to work for Ted Turner, whose visions have been and still are limitless . . . a man who launched the world's first live, in-depth, round-the-clock, all-news network, one of the most important events in journalistic history. CNN has become the most significant and most talked-about television service in the world. Ted Turner revolutionized the communications industry, and I consider it a blessing to be a part of it.

To my friend Hal Gulliver, former editor of the *Atlanta Constitution*, who spent months with me going over every chapter with his fine editorial pen and journalistic sense and extracting personal glimpses and anecdotes that I seemed slow to remember, I offer immense thanks.

My profound thanks to the great people at Longstreet Press, including Chuck Perry, President and Editor, John Yow, Associate Editor, and Michelle Wright, Publicist.

I respectfully acknowledge the photographic talents and contributions of the photographers whose works are included in this text: H. S. Rhoden, Beth Hoffman, Kelly Mills, General Davis, Jessie Sampley, Count Jackson, William Hollins, Granville Allen, Artmen Photographic Studio, Dev O'Neil, Ella Hamlin, Joe Potts, Elaine Tomlin, Harmon Perry, *Dollars & Sense Magazine*, Beverly Swanagan, Delta Airlines, and the official photographer for the White House.

FOREWORD

For those of us who served the social revolution of the sixties and since, this book will generate more than one tear, more than one smile; as for those who did not participate, it will take them backstage to see the workings of the movement through the eyes of one keenly involved. The author, however, never tries to lay a guilt trip on anyone or to make anyone fighting mad.

This doesn't surprise me, knowing Xernona Clayton and having been involved with her in a few projects over the years. There may be no more unassuming activist who yet produced such proud results. She is humble about it all, but she writes in detail of her accomplishments.

Like the coiffure which has long been her trademark, this trip through civil rights struggles and high-level business activities is precise, orderly, and proper. Xernona attracts the attention and commands the respect of others in any gathering, and this recollection of her involvement with civil rights leader Martin Luther King, Jr., Ku Klux Klan Grand Dragon Calvin Craig, entertainer Duke Ellington, Pulitzer Prize-winning publisher/editor Ralph McGill, business mogul Ted Turner, Ambassador Andy Young, and others renowned for diverse accomplishment will reinforce the respect for her by her friends past and build anew from this book's readers.

Although the autobiography includes joyful childhood anecdotes, and some impressive experiences as a confidante to one of the world's richest and most powerful entrepreneurs, its main thrust has us marching through reforms in human relations. For those of us who acknowledge there is yet much undone in eradication of inequities and prejudices, we have a litany here of one struggle and achievement after another resulting in an improved state in the lives of millions.

Just as she disarmed Ku Kluxer Craig, Xernona will win

over your heart no matter what your philosophy. This petite, pretty, and decorous person exudes a positive attitude toward whatever she undertakes. However, she is the epitome of Teddy Roosevelt's soft-spoken soul carrying a big stick, for she uses such power as may be necessary to get the job done.

It's both enjoyable and insightful when our author shares her father's ministerial manner. In hearing of her family we better understand why she is of such good character. She has indeed marched a lifetime, and with genteel demeanor. She is compassionate and forgiving; she is devoid of ego; she is intelligent and charming; she has the highest of morals, unimpeachable integrity, and impeccable grooming. Underneath such a profile this package of dynamite is quite well camouflaged . . . which puts her one up in every encounter.

She describes her personal involvement in situations of international importance — from the King assassination in Memphis to the Goodwill Games in Moscow — and tells us with just as much emphasis of individual (mostly unreported) victories: integrating the employment of a Jewish-owned Chicago liquor distributor; breaking through racial barriers in the millinery department of Louisville's leading department store; eliminating the "white only" society news rule at the *Atlanta Constitution*; opening public hospital services to people of all races nationwide.

She moves on her own, or with a group. She supported the work of the Urban League, the Southern Christian Leadership Conference, the NAACP, and the American Friends Service Committee, and represented each on different occasions.

She helped the Model Cities program in Atlanta and the school dropout program in Los Angeles, and she coerced toughies in street gangs and the honorable Georgia Commissioner of Labor to meet together for productive employment opportunities. She marches for the cause of justice and equality.

Dubbed "the Communicator" by McGill, this "straight-laced" friend of mine makes me proud of the human race.

She illustrates how one person can make a difference. But is she just one person? Being a twin she admits to, but we see independent dedication and commitment to the social, civic, religious, political, academic, journalism, and business communities — each to a degree of overwhelming proportions!

While I was president of the Atlanta City Council (then called the Board of Aldermen) and mayor of this city, I lived much of this era with Xernona. When she would tell people, "Let's reason together," she was just as willing to listen as she was to push her point. Her part in history proves you can achieve change and still have each side feel the other is reasonable. She caused few confrontations but many concurrences.

We have all benefited by the charity in her heart and soul. Let's hope many others take their marching orders from her cue. This book can help cause just such an inspiration.

Sam Massell
President, Buckhead Coalition, Inc.
Mayor, City of Atlanta, 1970-1974

One

The last time I saw Dr. Martin Luther King, Jr., alive was a plateau in my life, dividing the important things that came before and those that came after. I drove him to the Atlanta airport for his last flight to Memphis, just before he was killed.

It was already a hard, sad time for me. My husband, Ed Clayton, was a journalist who had moved to Atlanta from Los Angeles to work with Dr. King at the Southern Christian Leadership Conference, and I became increasingly involved in that work too. Ed had been executive editor of *Jet* magazine, and he was wonderful at helping Dr. King with his speeches and in putting out press releases and other SCLC publications. He was a highly talented journalist, a vigorous and energetic man, so it was all the more a shock when he died relatively young just over a year before.

Ed and I were already close to Martin and Coretta King and Mama and Daddy King, but the Kings were all especially good to me after Ed's death, making me feel truly part of their family.

That was how I came to take Dr. King to the airport for that last flight to Memphis. In fact, I had also driven him to the airport a few days before for an earlier flight to Memphis.

This was unusual in that Coretta almost always drove him to the airport. He had a driver for most of the appointments on his busy schedule, but Coretta liked driving him to the airport. It gave her a special private time with him and she enjoyed it. But she was recuperating from minor surgery and was confined to her home for a while, so she asked me if I would take over.

Sometimes you remember things in a distorted way because of what happened later, but I am sure I remember this accurately. I recall picking Dr. King up at his home that day, and I remember the children seeming apprehensive, even though they were accustomed to his leaving on trips. Maybe they sensed their father's mood. Or maybe they had heard something on the news about Dr. King and Memphis. Violence had erupted there during a demonstration he had participated in a few days earlier. Dr. King said in the car that he was going to have to find a way to spend more time with the children.

He was feeling gloomy about that particular mission that afternoon. The earlier march, on behalf of the sanitation workers, had been suspended because of the violence, and Dr. King came back to Atlanta, feeling unhappy about the whole thing. I remember he came by my house to tell me how depressed he was about the violence. It looked, he said, as if things had changed in the country, as if the mood and tenor of the country were shifting and not in a good direction. "Something is happening," he said; "I don't understand exactly what but something is happening."

I had never seen him so restlessly pondering over any one situation. He used the phrase "planted violence." A man had been killed in the march in Memphis, and Dr. King told me he believed the violence had been planned. Of course, there had been violence and even death in earlier civil rights demonstrations, but Dr. King said that this was the first time he felt that someone ostensibly part of the march itself had deliberately "planted" violence. Because of that, he told me, he was rethinking plans for our summer project, the Poor People's March on Washington. I know that others who were close to Dr. King believed later that he would have wanted that project to continue, and maybe he would have, but I also know that a few days before his death he told me, "I'm convinced I'm not going to go through with it."

He was going to take at least a year off for a sabbatical, he said, perhaps even two years. "I will take Coretta and we will go to Sweden or to Switzerland or to India or somewhere," he told me, "and I am going to meditate about what we need to do from this point on."

At this time, too, Dr. King was deeply concerned because of American involvement in the war in Vietnam. He had taken a strong public stand against our involvement and had lost many friends and supporters as a result. Even some close friends turned against him, including one woman in New York who had been a substantial fundraiser and had become a personal friend of the King family. She was the wife of a doctor, a socialite and an activist, supportive in the past of almost everything Dr. King did. She was a key figure not only because she could raise money but because she could also get other people of influence to help. But she simply did not share his view on Vietnam.

It was an agonizing period for him, a time of tremendous pain and suffering. He understood he would be criticized when he spoke out on Vietnam, but I think he believed that his close friends and supporters would still stand by him. Many did, of course, but many pulled away from him, so he was very down at this point. And he was worried, too, because fundraising was more difficult. People were not contributing as they once had, and you could certainly tell the difference in the SCLC coffers.

Yet Dr. King was not totally gloomy even in those difficult days. In fact, one Sunday not long before that last trip to Memphis was a most happy occasion. I was over at his home that afternoon with just family — Martin and Coretta and his mother Alberta King—and somehow we all started sitting around the piano talking, reminiscing about old times.

Dr. King used to like to tease me sometimes, and he said to me that day, "You don't really know that I can sing, do you?" I admitted it: "No, I really don't know that, Dr. King." "Yes, I can really sing," he insisted. "I used to sing with my mother." Well, his mother was right there, and she explained that when Martin was a little boy she used to play for differ- ent churches—Daddy King's church, of course, but also churches in neighboring communities and nearby towns. Mrs. King did not have a regular babysitter, she said, so she would often take young Martin along with her, and, when she would start playing and the choir would sing, he would chime in.

Then Coretta, an excellent singer with professional train- ing, began kidding him about whether he could still sing. But he insisted, "I'm *still* good." He knew that I played the piano, so he said, "You sit down and strike up a tune, and I'll show you how good I am."

Well, I sat down and accompanied him on an old gospel hymn, and then we all got to singing. One song led to another, and pretty soon Mama King took over the piano. It became an old-fashioned gospelfest, the greatest time. His mother seemed so happy, almost delirious because we were all having such a good time.

I remember, too, how he teased me on that drive to the airport. People at the Southern Christian Leadership Con- ference ended up doing those things they did best, and because I was regarded as a good organizer, I spent my time contacting people and putting things together for programs and projects, getting people involved. Dr. King knew that and he valued it. I organized the last big annual SCLC convention that Dr. King attended, the last one before his death, and he was so pleased with the way everything went that he told the board of directors afterward he wanted me to plan and orga- nize every annual meeting.

But he would tease me because I was not ordinarily involved in demonstrations, and on that ride to the airport he asked, "Xernona, when are you going to come march with me?"

"Dr. King," I answered, "I've been marching all the time." He nodded and laughed.

I believe that is true of my life, through a lot of different kinds of experiences: growing up in Oklahoma in what I knew was a racially segregated community, yet not suffering there any of the more overt forms of discrimination; going to my first job after college in Chicago, where my twin sister and I worked for the Urban League on job discrimination; facing the bitter side of segregation in a really personal sense when the biggest department store in Louisville did not want to let me try on a black hat I needed to wear to my father-in-law's funeral; working with Dr. King; helping run the Model Cities program in Atlanta and making a curious new friend, the former Grand Dragon of the Georgia Ku Klux Klan; becoming the first black person to host a television program in the South; helping Coretta King through the hard days immediately after Dr. King's death; joining Ted Turner's communications empire and becoming part of the Good Will Games in Moscow; finding that being "disinvited" to speak to a local women's group, when they discovered I was black, could open other doors, including an invitation to speak to the national convention of the same group.

And, yes, always trying to do those things that carry on Dr. King's dream. I think I can honestly say, *I've been marching all the time.*

Two

We lived directly across the street from a white school while I was growing up in Muskogee, Oklahoma, and yet my sister Xenobia, my brother James, and I walked several miles each day to get to a black school.

That was clearly unjust, and certainly even then, growing up in the 1940s, I was aware of segregation, but at that time we did not think a great deal about it. We walked several miles to our school and we had a wonderful time doing it, meeting our friends along the way, talking and joking, living the life given us. In fact, I was in my twenties before I encountered really mean-spirited racial discrimination aimed directly at me.

My father was a Baptist minister who was known and respected in the white community as well as the black. The mayor would come to our house, the chief of police, the leaders and pillars of the white community. My father's counsel and influence were often called upon. Also, most every politician wanted to have Daddy's endorsement since my father was a significant figure in the black community, though Muskogee's black population was relatively small.

Almost everyone respected my father as an honest person.

He did not give unsolicited advice, but he would give you an answer when you asked for it. He was a softspoken man and never raised his voice; he was quiet and very thoughtful. I realize now what a virtue that is, but it frustrated us children when he would ponder his answers to our requests for what seemed like a long time.

We would often challenge my mother in the household when we were children. She might say, "Go wash the dishes," and my sister and I would reply sweetly, "In just a minute" and go on doing what we wanted to do. But Daddy was one who believed in having some order. We could delay and delay with Mother, and Daddy would let us play out our little scene until he got tired of it. Then we would see that foot tapping—the only sign he ever showed of irritation—and everybody would go skedaddling to do what we were supposed to do.

As an example of my father's influence in the community, I remember once when the judge called him about a young black man, a teenager about fourteen or fifteen who had been in trouble a lot with the law, one scrape after another. Nothing really serious, not murder or anything like that, but serious enough. So the judge called my father and said he wanted to come by and talk to him about this young man. The judge figured my father knew the young man's family, and he asked Daddy for advice.

After sitting and talking with the judge for a long time, Daddy recommended that the judge give the boy to his grandmother, telling her that if he got into trouble again then she would be accountable. But my father also advised that the judge first counsel the grandmother to see if she felt she could control her grandson's behavior, put the question to her and see what her reaction would be. The boy's mother, frankly, was a weak parent, and the grandmother did go down and talk to the judge and agree to accept responsibility for her grandson. Of course the judge never told the grandmother that he had talked to Daddy about it; those consultations were always confidential. But the grandmother did assume control, and the young man graduated from high school without ever having another scrape with the law.

My father had three children by a first marriage. Following his first wife's death, he met and later married my mother, and they had four children—my older sister Vera first, my brother James four years later, and then Xenobia and me, the twins. My father's first three children—Fred, Mary, and Selena—were considerably older than we were, and so *their* children—Robert, Lorene, Clotiel, and Wynona—were much closer to our ages, our contemporaries. They were literally our nieces and nephews, but we loved each other as close members of the same family, in warm continuity.

My mother was one-quarter Cherokee Indian, and she had an Indian's contemplative nature. She was quiet and very deep in her thinking. She observed long and hard before she made a friend. Someone might come to the house several times, and mother would stare and think, slow with her words and her warmth, but once she sized it all up and decided that it was all right, then she became a very good friend. She was never outgoing, though, and quite the opposite of my hugely gregarious father. My mother was definitely a homebody.

Mother belonged to that old female tradition of doing everything for her family. She washed and ironed and starched Daddy's shirts. She washed and ironed all of our clothes. She cleaned the house, constantly. She cooked a real meal for dinner every day—never snacks, but dinner. Sunday dinner typically included fried chicken, mashed potatoes, green peas, and Waldorf salad. We loved that Waldorf salad because it was a Sunday special, not something we got during the week. She would prepare *somebody's* favorite dessert each week. She would ask ahead of time, whose favorite is it going to be this week? We would take turns, so one week it would be sweet potato pie, the next might be raisin pie, and the next week lemon. Mother herself loved coconut cake, so I think maybe we had coconut cake more often that anything else.

Mother was meticulous. The table was always set with a pretty tablecloth and good plates, never paper. I picked that up from her; I don't like an undressed table.

Curiously, mother did not teach us much about housework as we were growing up. She wanted to do all the chores as the woman of the house and didn't require much of us. The only time we even washed dishes was when she was really tired, maybe after a long day, and she would tell us we were just going to have to do the dishes. She did not teach us how to cook or clean the house. My sister and I both grew up as self-sufficient persons, so I don't suppose we suffered any real harm, but I think it would have been nice to have learned how to do more things as we were growing up.

Mother tried to be a disciplinarian, yet my sister and I often knew how to finagle her, and we could usually tell if she really meant it when she said yes or no. Sometimes we misjudged, and if my mother decided that she had given the final word and we were not paying attention to her, she would do us violence. I mean, she switched us. There was a peach tree out in the backyard, and the small limbs of a peach tree make fine, long, limber, and very painful switches. Mother would always make us go get our own switches, and it was a long time before we realized that it was a mistake to choose the small limbs. She would switch us good, but she would be pleasant again right afterward and make plain that she was not angry any more. We hated her while the switchings were going on, and we always ended up loving her afterwards.

Mother was quite independent-minded. Our family was totally involved in the church, all of us except Mother, and that was most unusual. As I look now at the wives of ministers, I realize my mother was probably viewed by some as a misfit. She certainly was atypical. She rarely went to church. Usually the minister's wife has got to be there in church whether she wants to be or not, but Mother stayed home on Sundays and had our dinner ready when we came home. My sister, my brother, and I would go to Sunday school and church and then back to church again in the evening, but not Mother. Of course she did other things, like paying her dues to the Missionary Society and baking cakes and pies for church occasions, but she preferred to stay home and provide for the needs of her family. We were the most important people to her.

We were always ready to go home after church, too. There was such joy and happiness in our home that we really did not care what went on in other people's worlds, and our friends almost always came over to our house. My father was a great storyteller, and in the winter we would sit around the fire and listen to his stories. Meanwhile, Mother was always happy and good humored, always moving around, always cooking. There was the smell of good food in the house most of the time, not just in holiday seasons. Our nieces and nephews often visited with us and added to the family joy.

However, there was one bone of contention between my mother and my father. My father would often bring a visiting minister home for dinner, without warning, and I think Mother almost dragged him to divorce court over that, not literally but perhaps in her heart. In fact, we only saw our mother and father fighting one time while we were growing up, and that was the cause. It seems funny now looking back on it, but at the time it frightened us kids. It was towards the end of World War II when we were little, and because of the war many foodstuffs were rationed and you had to stand in line to buy them.

Mother prided herself on having a full pantry, on never running out of anything. We used to have flour, all the basic foodstuffs, rolls of toilet tissue, anything you needed regularly in the home. Including butter, which was particularly hard to come by.

At any rate, Daddy brought a minister home to spend the night, and mother cooked biscuits for breakfast and served the real butter. Not everybody had butter in those days, and this visiting minister appeared tickled to death to see that real butter on the table. He loved those biscuits and he kept eating them with such abundant gobs of butter that my mother got put out with him, even to the point of making a comment like "You are eating an awful lot of butter."

That was embarrassing, and my father believed that you should never embarrass or insult anybody if you could possibly help it, especially in your home. So when the visitor left, Mother and Daddy had a serious quarrel. Mother fussed at him about fussing at her and he fussed some more at her, a real encounter that seemed like the end of the world. We kids did not know anything about divorce because we did not know anybody who ever got a divorce, but Mother said something like, "If that's the way you are going to be, I'm going to leave." My sister and brother and I thought that meant they really were about to separate forever, and we cried and cried. But that conflict quickly passed, probably far less serious than we perceived at the time.

My mother's mother was half-Cherokee. We only saw her a few times because she died when we were young, but I remember she had very dark skin, while our mother had beautiful reddish, rich skin, like an Indian. Grandmother had long hair, really long silky hair, beautiful. She parted it in the middle, and it was so long that she could comb it in her lap and over her knees. Her hair was still naturally black and silky up until the day she died. My mother had long hair, too, though her hair turned gray in her later years, after she had a fever.

My sister and I remembered my grandmother from those few visits when we were young because she was a little eerie. She used to sit in the dark all the time and she would comb her long hair and watch us. She would not talk much but she seemed kind, and we were not afraid of her as children, just aware that she was a little different. My mother had some of that same distant characteristic.

We were really blessed, I think now looking back, blessed with a good home and good parents who counseled us and loved us as they fed and took care of us. My father always reminded us that you cannot control the superficial things but you can control how you think and how you feel about other people.

Three

My father was definitely the strongest influence in my early life; he was the stabilizer for all of us in the family. We lived in a small town, and our economic status probably defined us as poor because my father was a Baptist minister and my mother did not work, but I never knew I was poor. Many things happened that should have made us realize my father's strength, but you don't analyze such things while you are living through them.

My sister and I were growing up at a time when black people were going through this phase of judging whether their hair was "good" or not. My sister and I were thought to have good hair, and the fact that it was long was also considered special. So we were twins and we were described as cute little girls with good, long hair. Everybody told us, aren't you lucky? You are so cute and you have such good hair. We heard that three times each day, every day of our young lives, from year one. We grew up on that—"aren't they cute?" If we had not had the kind of strong father we did have, we would have believed all that up until right now, thinking how cute we were and how wonderful that we had good hair.

Our father brought us back to reality. He would say, "I

don't understand these people who have such weighty opinions on frivolous things. I am not sure I know what they mean by good hair. Everybody's hair is good if you wash it and clean it. If you do that, your hair will be good." Then he would say, "People keep talking about how you are twins and how wonderful that is; well, you didn't choose to be twins, so you don't deserve any compliments for that."

He always made sure to minimize all those superficial traits people kept telling us were so wonderful. "Those are frivolous things," he would tell us, "because those are things over which you have no control; you didn't choose any of that." Then, he would slip in something about our being black, the color of our skin. "You didn't choose the color of your skin," he would say. "You didn't choose your sexual identification. You didn't choose to be twins. You didn't choose the texture of your hair. Don't let people fool you; that's frivolous stuff." So we grew up learning that those things were not so important. Daddy taught us that what you can control is how you feel about yourself inside and how you treat other people, how you treat your fellow man. That's where you need to put your effort, he said, when you look in the mirror and analyze who you are and what you are doing.

Our father cared deeply about education, and it saddened him that he felt he had done so little for the education of his children. His first wife died in childbirth, and his first children were much older than we. He was truly struggling economically at that earlier time and did not get a chance to educate his children for financial reasons. His second marriage produced four children. Our older sister Vera was eight years older than we were, a very pretty girl and very nice, a big sister we loved and admired. Daddy hoped to send her on to college, but she wanted to get married. She literally married the boy next door, our next-door neighbor, so our father never got a chance to send her to college. The next child, our older brother James, was drafted into military service in 1944. Daddy was able to use his influence to get James deferred at least until he could finish high school, but because of getting sidetracked into military service he ended up never going to college. So my sister and I, the youngest children, were Daddy's last chance. He used to pray all the time, and we used to hear him pray, that the good Lord would just let him live long enough to see us get through college. He really wanted to see us get that college education. The good Lord must have heard his prayer because we graduated from Tennessee State University in June of 1952 and Daddy died six months later.

We came to attend Tennessee State because of a second father, our godfather you might say. Our father was active in the National Baptist Convention, and by going to all those meetings with him we came to know a man named Dr. Henry Allen Boyd. He was a wealthy man with an only daughter, and I suppose he was one of those fathers who want their little girl to stay a little girl forever. When reality came and she grew up and got married, I think he felt he had lost his whole world. He met us one year when we were just little tykes attending the Baptist Convention with our father, and he seemed to fall in love with us. He came to my father and said, "Look, I want those kids; I want to adopt them." Daddy did not take any of that seriously, but Dr. Boyd did become almost like another father, and when we got ready for college he urged our father to let us come to college in Nashville, where he lived.

Dr. Boyd was a minister but also a businessman, head of the National Baptist Convention, whose publishing house was big business. He was also president of Citizens Trust Bank in Nashville and served on several boards. He had also inherited some money and property from his father, so he was very, very wealthy. He told my father that if we would come to Nashville he would help us whenever we needed help, that Daddy would never have to worry about money or anything, that he would take care of us.

Actually, we were thinking of going to Florida A&M University in Tallahassee. We had gotten a small scholarship offer to attend the college in Nashville but a bigger offer to attend Florida A&M. The president of Florida A&M at that time was Dr. William Gray, the father of Congressman William Gray from Philadelphia. Dr. Gray was a Baptist minister, and after meeting us at the Baptist convention he had offered us a scholarship to attend Florida A&M. We finally had a little family conference, and Daddy said that since Dr. Boyd wanted us so much to come to Nashville we probably would be happier there, because if anything went wrong he would be like another parent. Also, we knew Dr. and Mrs. George W. Gore, who were extremely kind from the time we met them and helpful to us throughout our college years. So we decided on Nashville.

We were a close family and we all loved each other, but my sister and I loved our father especially. My mother's favorite was James, her only son. My older sister Vera was an only child for four years, so of course my mother and father loved her, but then she started to grow up. My sister and I were the babies when we came along, and we were the apple of our father's eye. We loved him so, we could literally smell his presence in the house.

After we went away to college, we would telephone home to report anything that we achieved. We were sure of encouragement from home, and we loved getting Daddy's approval of the good things we did. Of course, we also learned along the way not to expect support for any bad things we might do, and we knew we could never fool or trick him. An incident from when I was twelve years old had taught me that lesson forever.

I had begun to play the piano when I was about nine, and when I was twelve my father commented one day, "You're doing pretty well." Then he added, "We're going to need somebody to play at the church." This was a great compliment to me, a thrill, and I told my father I would love to play for the church, his church. He impressed on me that it would be a big responsibility for someone just twelve years old, and I assured him I could do it. I always felt that I was mature for my age at every stage of my life, and so when my father went on to caution me about not missing rehearsals and taking the task seriously, I said again, "Daddy, I can do it." So he gave me the opportunity, and the church paid me four dollars each week to play for the choir.

Then came the Sunday I will always remember. Our neighbors the Grant Smiths had two daughters, Ella Jean and Bobbie Lee, who were close friends of ours. Now, the Smiths went to church regularly, but on this particular Sunday Mr. Smith, who owned an automobile tire shop, had to make a business trip over to Tulsa to pick up something for a customer. He asked his family to ride with him, and then Ella Jean asked him if we could ride along too. Daddy had already gone to church because he always left earlier than we did, and so my sister and I told our mother that we were going to go to Tulsa with the Smiths, and she said that was all right. I don't claim I had really forgotten about playing the piano at the church, but I managed to put it out of my head. My mother probably didn't think of it at all, since we didn't say how long we would be gone.

Xenobia and I went on to Tulsa and had a wonderful time and did not get back home until late afternoon. Daddy had already come home and then gone back to the church for the evening service, so we did not see him until about nine o'clock that night.

He called us into the living room, which we always dreaded because that was what he would do when he wanted to give us a lecture. He would tell us to have a seat, quite formally, and he sat in this big chair with us on the floor right in front of him.

"Well, did you have fun today?" he inquired, and at first we thought he was simply asking about our day. I burst out in jubilation, "Oh yes, Daddy, we had a great time."

Then came the lecture. It was nice that I had fun, he said, but I had not shown up at church to play the piano. "I'm going to ask you to consider something," he said. "Imagine a scale. On one side you have twenty-six members of your church choir. Consider the balance here. These members of the choir were expecting you to show up. They had to get ready to show up themselves, and they had families, so you multiply that twenty-six by two, their spouses, and then say most of them had children and they had to get their children ready early in order to come to the choir on time." Then Daddy threw in the congregation which had been counting on me, and he threw in himself, the pastor, and when he got through he had, oh, a cast of thousands.

All of these people had been counting on me, expecting me to show up, he said. "On this imaginary scale," he went on, "you have five hundred people on one side of the scale and just you on the other side. You had a good time today," he said specifically to me, since my sister had not pledged to be there to play the piano, "but the price was the inconvenience and sacrifice and sense of imposition of all those five hundred people. One person has fun, while everybody else suffers. When you take on responsibility," he told me, "when you give your word, your word has got to have meaning. You have to be on time if that is your responsibility. If you are late or don't show up, you are showing a disregard and total disrespect for everybody else. Until you learn that," he said, "you have not assumed any real sense of responsibility."

"Remember," he said, "even if you give your word to somebody that you are going to meet them at high noon on the street corner to count the cars going by, something unimportant, you still must show up on time because it is a reflection on your character when you ever run late or fail to show."

It was a lasting lecture, obviously one I've never forgotten. To this day I am extremely punctual and reliable. My father taught me a great many other things as I was growing up, and I remember one other lesson that had lasting impact. I wish he were still here today so that I could tell him how important his lessons were.

We had a wealthy cousin, my mother's niece, who lived in Oklahoma City. Her husband was a doctor, and she was a teacher, and they had oil wells on their property. My mother had taken care of her mother, Beulah Stewart, in her last illness, and she had ultimately died in our house while my mother was looking after her. So our cousin Willie felt indebted to my mother and was always doing things for us, the twin girls. Every Christmas when we were small we got every kind of doll you can imagine, from Betsy Wetsy to dolls short and tall. Most little girls might get one doll for Christmas, but our cousin would send us dolls by the numbers. At Easter she would send us Easter outfits, not just one but one of every color, pink and blue and yellow.

Our best friend then was an illegitimate girl who lived nearby. She was also the daughter of an illegitimate child; in fact, there were three generations of illegitimacy. That did not matter to us because she was our friend, but she and her family were truly poor, much poorer than we were. When Christmas came they had hardly anything; the household simply could not afford anything.

So this one Christmas we had dressed up and were each carrying one of our new dolls around when Daddy asked, "Which one of your new dolls are you going to give your friend?" We could not believe our ears. "These are our new things," we told our father. "We can't give away our new dolls."

So Daddy gave us a lecture on friendship: "If you've got a friend," he said, "you share with your friend whatever you have."

He made us give our really poor friend a doll that Christmas and later a new dress at Easter. At first this was a painful lesson in sharing, but we discovered that it didn't kill us. We had three or four new dresses left and new dolls left, and our friend was happy with her one doll and had on a new dress, too. In fact, each year it got less painful. That first day, the first time our father proposed that idea, we thought he had gone lunatic on us, but giving to others became a habit, and to this day Xenobia and I are both very sharing people.

Four

My sister and I headed for Chicago after college, to our first real jobs as undercover agents for the Urban League. That sounds more dangerous than it really was, as if I were a spy for the FBI; the danger we faced was more along the lines of being embarrassed and treated with discourtesy.

My father was so proud that we had both completed college, that he had finally educated two of his children, and he was proud of me too because I had gotten a scholarship to the University of Chicago. That was really why we went to Chicago, because of my scholarship, but school wouldn't start until the fall, so we got jobs with the Urban League for the summer.

The Urban League wanted us to be guinea pigs. They were trying to find out where the job barriers were in the city, where employers discriminated based on color. Most of the larger companies were hypocritical about it; they did discriminate in hiring but pretended they did not. The Urban League was pressing them to live up to what they professed and really hire qualified minority members.

This was in the summer of 1952, a time when the Urban League was a great source of employment for black people.

They held career conferences in black colleges where one could meet people from various companies, and when we knew we were going to Chicago, we let the Urban League there know. We asked them to let us know if anything came along, and that was when they asked us to be guinea pigs.

Actually, we already had some Urban League contacts in Chicago: Executive Director Lemuel Pemberton and Leroy Jeffries, advertising director for Johnson Publishing Company. They took us under their wings when we first got to the city, helping us meet people, even helping us find an apartment, and it was their idea to put us to work for the Urban League. "We're helping you," they said, "and we've got this little project going and so you can help us."

My sister and I both had college degrees and we looked like young people ready to go to work. Some people based their discrimination on the belief that black folk did not want to work, that they were just lazy, but we even looked like we had "get up and go." We were clean and we dressed neatly, and we had basic office skills and good diction. If nothing else, we could certainly answer the telephone in proper fashion. Either of us could have become a receptionist or a secretary or a filing clerk, all of those kinds of basic jobs. And if the advertisements for these jobs also called for a college degree, we had that covered, too.

The point was that a lot of companies would not hire black people for these jobs, and the Urban League was trying to break down such racial barriers. Some were major companies, like the famed department store Marshall Field's and Illinois Bell. Their ads might say something like: Office worker wanted, light typing, neat appearance. Someone from the Urban League would call the company and ask, is this job still available? If the answer were yes, my sister and I would hurry over and apply for the job in person. We would usually arrive only minutes after the telephone call, and then the office manager would see that we were black and say, "Oh my, I just filled that job." We went through several of these experiences.

Yet we did not really feel that rejection personally. It did not hit us so strongly because we anticipated what might happen and we knew the Urban League was trying to change things, and they had a definite mission and purpose. Somehow we rationalized that those companies were not turning us down personally, maybe because we knew we were doing it for the Urban League. However, we did feel the pain of that racial rejection.

We even ended up with some job offers. Alden's, a mail-order house opened up for us. Spiegel opened up for us. Illinois Bell changed its mind. These companies all rejected us at first, then called back and were willing to offer us jobs.

The choice we ended up making came from an experience that started out like some of the other rejections. It was a Jewish firm, Sunset Inc., a liquor distributing firm. It seemed ironic that we ended up there, since our father was a minister. We were never around liquor when we were growing up.

But let me explain why we took the job at Sunset. We went there for an interview after the Urban League told us that this was a company that had never hired a black person. The two co-owners, Sydney Waller and Marvin Coleman, are still important names for me. They apparently felt, perhaps because they were Jewish, that if it were possible to change racial discrimination against blacks, they wanted to be among those helping make such changes. Someone heard them make such a statement, so the Urban League thought they might be disposed to open doors by changing their own hiring practices.

They had run an ad for a bookkeeper. I didn't have any of those skills but my sister was trained in bookkeeping, so we went there together to answer that ad. The woman who interviewed us said, "Oh, I think we have already filled that position."

She was nice about it but it was clearly a rejection. "There must be a mistake," she said, "because we really have promised that job to one of the ladies in the firm. I'm sorry you have wasted the time coming by here." Mr. Waller and Mr. Coleman happened to come in from lunch while we were being rejected, and when they saw us, they called the interviewer into their office. That office had windows, and though we couldn't hear anything, we could see some serious talk and a lot of gesturing. It turned out that they told her to ask if one of us could handle the bookkeeping job and then hire the other one of us as their receptionist. "We'll take them both," they said, as we learned later.

The woman interviewer came back out, and this time she said, "I'm afraid I got fouled up again. Those were the owners and they say we have not really *promised* the book-keeper's job to anybody, and, as a matter of fact, we also have another opening for a receptionist." At this point I was not even sure if I really wanted to take the job because it was getting into the summer and I was going to graduate school soon. But this seemed important, breaking down these barriers, and I decided to take the job and work at it as long as I could.

We checked back with the Urban League and told them about being offered jobs at Sunset, and, believe it or not, that was when they told us that Alden's had called us back and also Illinois Bell. We went back by the office and had a great time talking about how we now had real job choices.

Most of the people who turned us down were fairly nice about it, but there was one memorable exception. My sister and I have never forgotten the look on the woman's face at Marshall Field's. First a secretary announced us to a woman, all quite formal, and then we were escorted to the woman's office. The woman who asked us to be sent in was on the telephone when we got to her office and had her back to the door. "Be right with you," she said, but she didn't turn around and she stayed busy on the telephone for a short while. Then she wheeled around and saw us face to face, and the shock in her face was most apparent. "Are you sure they told you the receptionist's job was open?" she asked. "Because we filled that yesterday." Then she turned nice and said that she was just so sorry, but Xenobia and I always remembered that look of shock on her face when she saw that we were black.

Most people just lied to conceal their discriminatory policies, but I remember one woman at Illinois Bell who was really blatant about it, even though she was friendly in a personal way. She told us that the company had never really hired any black people. We were applying for service representatives jobs, for which you had to have a college degree, and they had advertised that there were several openings. We told her that we both had college degrees and that we thought we could get along well with almost anybody. "Of course you are free to apply," she told us, as if she really wanted us to understand that she was not turning us down because of race. But, she said, there were several other people working to fill the positions, and she needed to talk to them to see what was going on. "Let me just check," she said, and then she came back and told us in a very friendly voice that all the jobs had been filled. Surprise, surprise. "You probably would not have been happy here anyway," she said.

We got the message.

The Urban League also worked with black employees to try to change things from within. Some companies which did have black employees were reluctant to hire blacks for other positions. A black man at Alden's, Mr. William Bradshaw, was probably the one who helped persuade them to reconsider, and Mrs. Ada, a black woman at Spiegel, was trying to get them to change. The Urban League would encourage these black employees to urge their managers to change their policies on hiring, and some companies did change.

The Urban League helped us decide on Sunset, thinking that it was a better case than some. It was a smaller company, and, since the owners had personally made the decision to hire us, the Urban League thought they could probably use that as a good example for later. It might help persuade other owners to change their policies on hiring.

This was in the early 1950s, when most restaurants were still completely segregated. We noticed when we first started working at Sunset that people would pair off for lunch. Nobody ever asked us along and my sister and I ended up going to lunch with each other. We didn't really feel that the other employees were prejudiced against us or that they were being evil and ugly, because they weren't being evil. They would speak to us. They just wouldn't invite us to lunch.

But then came inventory night, the first one after we started working at Sunset. Everybody stayed late on this evening and just kept working until we finished, usually about eight o'clock. Then, the custom was for the bosses to take everybody out to dinner. Somebody on the staff would recommend some good place, always a different place from the last time, and the bosses at Sunset seemed to look forward to taking everybody out to a good restaurant. That first inventory night of our time there, somebody recommended Ricardo's, then one of the best restaurants in Chicago.

The other people at Sunset had begun getting friendlier after we had been there only a short time, deciding, I guess, that we didn't bite, and everyone was in a good mood when we started for Ricardo's. There were about twenty people in our office, and our employers made reservations for the entire group. We got to the restaurant and had to wait for a long time. At first we did not realize what was happening, just that there seemed to be a lot of conversation going on, first with the maitre d' talking to Mr. Coleman and Mr. Waller and then with two other men, maybe managers, coming over to talk. We thought at first that the party was so big they were having problems with the table, but we soon found out that we were the problem, two little "black spots" in the group.

They were simply not going to seat a group with two young black women in it. We could not hear the conversation but there was a lot of consultation. We learned later that Mr. Coleman and Mr. Waller pulled out all the stops. They both belonged to several clubs, and they told the manager that if they were turned away they would see to it that none of these clubs ever used that restaurant again. The managers must have finally decided they had no choice. We did not plan it exactly, but we became the first black people to eat at Ricardo's.

Another good story from that summer at Sunset concerns a woman who worked there from Cicero, Mildred Konovsky. Cicero was a city infamous for its anti-black feeling, a place where serious race riots had occurred, and this woman came from a Cicero redneck environment, but she ultimately became our good friend. She loved to tell us about her family.

Both her mother-in-law and her brother-in-law lived with her, along with her husband Arthur. We were fascinated to learn that her brother-in-law had had the hiccups for seven years. But we were more personally interested in the mother-in-law. Mildred told us flatly that her mother-in-law hated black people, even though the family had a black maid who came each day.

This is almost funny, even though I suppose it really is not. Mildred gave us this example of how much her mother-in-law had kept old traditions of prejudice in her heart. A previous black maid got drunk on duty one day, and instead of changing the mother-in-law's bed, she decided to climb in and take a nice nap. When the mother-in-law came and found the maid there, she was so angry that she threw the maid out of the house and then burned the mattress. She had to buy all new bedclothes and a new mattress; the alternative — sleeping on the same mattress where the black maid had passed out — was simply unthinkable. Mildred said she wanted to invite us out to her house some evening, but she did want us to know what kind of mother-in-law she had. We came to have a pretty good sense of her mother-in-law.

Mildred's brother-in-law, the one who had the hiccups for so long, got even more ill that summer and finally died. She had not yet invited us to her home by that time, but she did very much want us to come to the brother-in-law's funeral. To be exact, she wanted us to come to the family hour in the funeral parlor one evening. Now we had read about the Cicero race riots, but they had occurred before we got to Chicago. Also, reading about something is one thing; experiencing it firsthand is another. So we went to the funeral parlor with the feeling that we were going under very personal circumstances to grieve with a friend, paying our respects as anyone would do.

We found our way to the funeral home without any difficulty, using the directions Mildred had given us. A funeral director greeted us at the door and asked, "May I help you?" There was no special anger in his tone, but it was as if he thought we were obviously in the wrong place. We told him we were looking for the Konovsky family, a private family gathering, and he told us there must be some mistake.

He never admitted to us that the Konovsky family was even there, just kept saying we had made a mistake. We had the name of the mortician and the name of the funeral home, so we were quite puzzled. How could there be any mistake? It was not an ugly confrontation, so at first it did not register on us that he was determined not to let us in. Finally we asked if we could use their telephone, thinking that somehow we really had gotten mixed up and that we should call the Konovsky home and see if anybody could give us better directions. The funeral director told us that they only had one telephone but there was a public phone down the street.

We realized then that the man was not being helpful, and it was beginning to dawn on us that he simply did not want us there. We tried to decide what to do, whether to look around for another funeral home in the area, or to just give up and leave and go home, thinking that we had at least tried to pay our respects. What we didn't know was that our friend, Mildred, had left the funeral home to go get something at home and was just on her way back. We ran into her as we started to leave.

We started to tell her what had happened, and she said, "Oh no, this is the right place," and just swept us in with her. So we spent time with Mildred and the family, and even the mother-in-law was very nice to us, seeming proud of the fact that we had come to pay last respects to her son. It ended up being a nice family gathering, and everybody embraced us warmly.

As we were leaving the funeral home we saw the funeral director again, absolutely looking like a dead person himself. He was extremely upset, and he later told Mildred that he would prefer that her family never use that funeral home again, that they had never had any black people there, that it was in violation of their policy, and that they absolutely objected to Mildred having brought us in. Mildred ended up taking up our cause, speaking up to this man fiercely. It was the funniest thing, because Mildred was one of the ones who seemed to reject us when we first started working at Sunset, but now that we had become friends she would not put up with anyone abusing us.

Five

My husband-to-be, Ed Clayton, tried to get me to pose for a centerfold in a bikini soon after I met him.

I said no.

I had finished working for the Urban League and begun teaching school.

My first day of teaching school was almost my last. I was assigned to a boys' high school, Tilden Tech, and initially to a class of sixteen- and seventeen-year-olds, boys but really young men also, and I had chosen, without thinking about it much, a favorite sweater and skirt. It was certainly not a provocative outfit, but the boys in that first class responded as if I were a movie sweater-girl, Betty Grable or somebody; they couldn't stop commenting and laughing and joking. I suppose it was not just the sweater but also that I was not much older than they were.

They were testing me, but they were good humored and friendly with all their seeming rudeness. I was scared to death, but I thought if I could just retain my poise and keep my own good humor that I would be able to treat those teenagers with courtesy and also with dignity. I was also sure that if I once lost control of that class, which seemed possible, my teaching career would be over before it got started.

Those boys gave me the longest day of my life. They whistled, they told me they thought I was sexy, they called me "Teach." They would say things like, "Hey, Teach, you're a foxy Teach. We're going to learn a lot in here." I managed to keep my composure, but I really was about to die. I kept watching the clock, wondering if the day would ever end, and thinking I would never wear that blue cashmere sweater again. Really I felt like crying.

After I got through the day, I went home and threw all my sweaters away, and the next day I wore a proper suit. The boys found out that I would not tolerate rude behavior, the jeers and the sneers and the flirting, and they ended up respecting me and liking me. I had managed to keep control. I learned later that this group of boys was considered pretty bad; in fact, I was offered that first job as a substitute because they had chased their former teacher out. I guess I managed to bluff those boys that first day, and before long I began getting production from them. It was a music class and they ended up doing well. I also got along with the other teachers, so despite that hard first day, I ended up with good ratings from my students and my associates.

That was important to me because in Chicago then it was hard to get a teaching job, no matter how many degrees you had. There were a lot of people who wanted those jobs, so when I interviewed at the end of the term with the Board of Education I was not sure if I would be offered another position. I was afraid the stern-looking man who interviewed me might tell me that there were no full-time openings for the new school year. But he was the one who told me that my group of teenagers had such a bad reputation and yet I had managed to relate to them somehow. He told me I had shown myself to be a successful teacher in a relatively short time.

I was still trying to do some graduate work, but he asked me if I could be available full-time, not just as a substitute. There was not a single full-time opening available, he told me, but in order to keep me the school system was willing to assign me to two schools, a morning in one school and then the afternoon in the other. To me that sounded ideal. They gave me travel time so that I would have an hour for lunch and also an hour for the necessary travel from one school to the other. I really liked having that break during the day, and I also liked having two sets of young children and two sets of school administrators.

This was in the mid-1950's, the time when the U.S. Supreme Court declared school segregation unconstitutional. Yet I am not sure the decision at the time had much impact on my mind or heart. The Chicago school system was actually practicing "separate but equal," and there were both white and black teachers in the schools where I taught. The schools were segregated, but that seemed merely a reflection of residential patterns. Most students simply went to the schools nearest where they lived, and it was the neighborhoods that were divided into white and black.

One rude awakening I had during this time was discovering that some white teachers liked being assigned to schools with black students because they considered it a soft assignment. I noticed that when the bell would ring to start class, a lot of the white teachers would stand out in the hall and talk, sometimes for a long time, in no hurry at all to go into the classroom. I came to realize that these white teachers were taking their time and wandering into class when it pleased them because they did not think they had much teaching to do, that these black youngsters were not going to learn anyway. Their attitude was, "Well, these kids aren't going anywhere and they aren't going to accomplish anything, so what difference does it make?" The truth was, they were depriving those kids.

The two schools where I taught were elementary, not high school, so the children were younger and I liked them a great deal. I learned new respect for young kids, and some maternal instinct in me really came out. Little children are just enamored with romance, and the man I was dating at the time would come pick me up each day after school. Of course, the little children in my class got to know his car, and this was a big thing for them, getting a glimpse of teacher's boyfriend. At the end of the school day, I would march them out to the end of the schoolyard and dismiss them there, and then they could do whatever they wanted, hang around and play, or turn a flip, or head for home. But what they wanted to do was hang around me and wait for my boyfriend. They would point to his car and say, "Teacher, ooooh, your boyfriend is here," and they seemed delighted to tell me about it. Then they would stand around and watch me go to the car and wait to see if I were going to kiss him or whatever. Oh, I can still remember how those little children loved knowing something about the romantic part of their teacher's life.

This particular romance finally fizzled out, and I told my boyfriend one evening that it clearly was not going to work out. He didn't want to accept that verdict, so he showed up at the school the next afternoon just as if we had not broken up the evening before. I walked right past him. I was just not going to get in his car. This threw the children a real curve. They ran after me saying, "Teacher, didn't you see him?" How intrigued they were to witness the end of a relationship!

To return to the story of my husband-to-be. My former boyfriend, the one who fascinated the schoolchildren so much, had once worked for the heavyweight boxing champion Joe Louis and still was very much into the fight world when I knew him. He took me to a big fight one night and then afterward a lot of people congregated at this one popular restaurant/lounge. That is where I first met Ed Clayton.

I was choir director of one of the largest Baptist churches in Chicago then, the South Shore Baptist Church, and I played for the choir every Sunday. I had a strong sense of my spiritual commitment, yet I was not sanctimonious. I enjoyed going to nightclubs even though I didn't drink or smoke. The thing was, whenever I went anywhere, including nightclubs, I would invite people to come to my church.

That bikini photo offer was a big surprise. Ed Clayton was the executive editor of *Jet* magazine then, a popular publication in black communities all over the United States. It was also popular among whites who had an interest in the black community. I know that during the hectic days of the civil rights movement white journalists told me over and over that they read *Jet* each week, almost like a Bible, because it had the most complete reporting anywhere about black entertainers, sports figures, civil rights leaders, and business people, good reporting on almost anyone prominent in black communities over the country. In fact, some white journalists confessed to us that they were embarrassed to have other people see them with a copy of *Jet*, so they would put it inside *Time* or some other magazine. But they read it. Anyway, at this party after the fight Ed told me that actually he had been meaning to contact me and my sister. He asked if we could come by his office and talk to him about doing a photo story he had in mind. This may sound vain, but his request did not surprise me especially, since my sister and I had become popular pretty quickly in Chicago, part of it I am sure because we were identical twins. We had gotten used to receiving attention in college; we often found ourselves in the college newsreel that ran in the local theaters every Saturday, and we were featured sometimes in magazines, so we had a high profile, you might say.

Jet was a very serious magazine in many ways, but it was also full of social gossip and lighter features. One of the most popular was the centerfold, which each week featured a sexy photograph of an attractive young woman in a bikini. Now, *Jet* wasn't trying to be a *Playboy*; this was the only feature like that in the whole magazine, but it really was popular. The bikini photo might be of a model or an actress or just some attractive office girl, but readers were always eager to see who was in the centerfold with her curvaceous figure showing.

Ed was courteous and nice when we first met him, and Xenobia and I readily agreed to come talk with him in his office. I remember, too, that I told him in the nightclub that I wanted to extend him an invitation as well, that I wanted him to come to my church sometime, and I told him I played the organ at the South Shore Baptist Church. He looked at me in surprise, as if not quite sure what to make of someone in a nightclub talking to him about going to church.

My sister and I went down to the *Jet* magazine offices, and, sure enough, Ed told us that the picture story he had in mind was for the two of us to pose in bikinis for that centerfold. He said he had never posed a pair of twins before and it would get a great response. I was firm in my own negative response, and I told him, no, thank you very much, but we would never consider that.

Ed could not believe me at first. "You know I'm talking about *Jet* magazine?" he said. "With a circulation of 350,000 every week?" I said I didn't know about the circulation but what difference did that make? He told me that *nobody* turned down *Jet* magazine, but I told Ed he would just have to put us down in his book as the first, because we simply were not going to pose in bikinis for his centerfold.

Still in disbelief, he demanded to know why not, so we told him that our father was a Baptist minister in Oklahoma, much respected, and he would be deeply offended. We also informed him that we simply did not want to expose our bodies in a magazine, that we just wouldn't do it. I reminded him that I was the choir director in my church and that I felt it was less than decent to display that much of one's body in a centerfold. That was the kind of thing my sister and I would leave to people who found it acceptable.

Ed told me later he thought all that was the most flippant response from any young girl he had ever encountered. People offered him money to be in the magazine. Some young women offered him their all to be the centerfold, and here my sister and I were turning it down. I told him as we left that we appreciated talking to him, even if we couldn't do his centerfold, and that I really hoped he would still find the invitation to come to my church appealing. As we left, Ed was still courteous but seemed put out. It was clear that nobody had ever rejected him like that before.

My inviting people to church often led to a certain excitement for the congregation. My friend connected with boxing introduced me to Sugar Ray Robinson, then middleweight champion of the world, and I invited Sugar Ray to come to church too. He gave me a funny look and said that in all his travels all over the country nobody had ever invited him to church. He would like to come. I offered to send a car for him, but he insisted on coming on his own. He brought another famous fighter with him, Jersey Joe Walcott. Our minister introduced them in church and told the congregation that they were there because I had asked them to come. And much to my surprise, the Sunday after I had turned down his centerfold offer, Ed showed up at church. In fact, Ed came back for several Sundays thereafter. The pastor later invited him to speak at Men's Day, our major annual event. The congregation was thrilled that Ed was going to be the speaker. He was such an important man, they said, that we had to have special planning for the event, and before I knew it they made me chairman.

Ed and I became good friends. He ended up running photos of me and my sister in the magazine anyway, both of us fully clothed, and he wrote a story about us to run with the pictures. There was no romance between us, though, no romantic interest on my part. I had a special boyfriend, and Ed had a wife. But it happened that my own personal relationship was fizzling out, my engagement coming to an end, and Ed started talking to me about his own domestic problems. Well, I was smart enough to know that every married man pretends to be unhappy at home when he wants to go for somebody else, so I did not quite believe that his marriage was on the rocks. I thought that was just another line, so I ignored him at first. But there were enough women trying for him, women in the community who had heard that his marriage was breaking up, and they were putting pressure on him, standing in line for him. I suppose I was the one most attractive to him because I was the only one not "after him." Since I had just been through a failed romance, I wasn't interested in men right then, and he found that state of mind appealing. Eventually I did start listening to his marriage woes, even if I didn't believe all of it at first.

It turned out that the things Ed told me were all true. He found me a good listener, and by this time I had a reputation as a person you could talk to confidentially. I did not gossip, did not tell people's business to other people. He learned that about me, and that's really why we began to become more intimate. He would call me on the phone and talk for hours, about the two children and how hard it was with a marriage breaking up. I was giving him advice and some comfort, I suppose, but I also let him know that I did not play around with married men. If that was where his conversations were leading, I said, he better find another shoulder to cry on, because I was not interested. I made it clear that my morals were high and that I was pretty straightlaced.

But Ed did separate from his wife and got divorced, and soon after that he asked me out. At last our romance began to blossom. It was a wonderful time. Living in Chicago had always been exciting for me, but it was even more so after I married Ed. We felt very much at home there. We were an integral part of the social, civic, and religious community.

Six

I was certainly aware of racial discrimination while growing up in Oklahoma and while working for the Urban League in Chicago, but I was a twenty-nine-year-old married woman when I first faced racial discrimination in a way that seemed personally hurtful. It was in Louisville, Kentucky.

Louisville was Ed's hometown, and his father was well known there. He was the first black alderman on the city council and one of the first black elected officials in the South. He was a good Christian man, well respected, and a real civic leader. Ed was close to his father, and I had come to love and admire my father-in-law.

We were still living in Chicago at this time, and when we heard that Ed's father was sick, we decided to drive down to cheer him up. We didn't think the illness was critical, so we planned only a short visit and packed very few clothes. But after we got there Ed's father got worse and worse and died within a short time. Unexpectedly, we found ourselves planning the funeral, doing all the things you have to do.

I was not much of a wearer of hats back then, but I thought it would be appropriate to wear a black hat to the funeral. At that time in Louisville, Stewart's was the leading department store; they had the finest merchandise, some of it very expensive. My father-in-law used to send us gifts on special occasions, and these gifts would typically come from Stewart's, so when I decided to get a black hat for the funeral, I went down to the only store I knew in Louisville.

I walked into Stewart's thinking I would not buy a terribly expensive hat because it was unlikely that I would ever wear the hat again after the funeral. They had a hat bar on the main floor with the less expensive hats, and I was standing at the counter with the other women looking at hats, and I noticed that the saleslady behind the counter was waiting on everybody but me. It did not occur to me at that moment that I was black and all the other women were white. I finally said, "Miss, could I see that hat right there?"

She reached for the hat I pointed to and then held it up. I thought she was asking, is this the one? I said, "Yes, that's it." She stayed behind the counter and just held the hat up, so finally I said, "Miss, may I see it? I want to try it on." She looked at me with utter scorn, but I still asked again, "Miss, may I see it? I want to try it on." She finally deigned to speak to me: "You know you can't try this hat on. What are you trying to do? Make trouble?" Then she threw the hat down.

It honestly hit me only then.

I looked around. All the other women looking at hats were white; everybody was white except me, including the saleslady. At first I wanted to turn and walk out, but then I said to myself, no, I can't do this. So I asked the saleslady if there were a buyer for hats in the store. Somehow I knew I wanted to report her to *somebody*, whether that helped anything or not. She wouldn't give me an answer, so I asked where the executive offices were and went upstairs to find them. I was upset, I know. "I want to talk to somebody, please," I said to the first person I saw.

This woman turned out to be very nice. I told her about what had happened, and I told her that I was in Louisville solely because of my father-in-law's illness and death, that I was from out of town, and that the only reason I had come to Stewart's was because it was the only store in Louisville that I knew by name. My father-in-law had had wonderful taste, I told her, and we had always been so pleased with the gifts he sent us from Louisville and they always came from this store.

The woman said she was really sorry and asked who my father-in-law had been. I told her, Mr. Eugene Clayton. His picture had been on the front page of the newspaper that day, a big picture on the front, and the lady exclaimed, "Oh, my goodness, Mr. Eugene Clayton."

I went on to tell her that I could not imagine that such a man could love a city as long as he did, could have lived there and loved it and contributed to it and embraced it, could have bought gifts for his family from this store, and now that same store prevented me from trying on a hat to wear to his funeral.

The woman apologized again—quite sincerely. She had someone from the executive offices escort me to the millinery department, which was actually on a higher floor, where the better hats were. I was introduced to the head of that department and told I should feel free to try on any hat of my choice. I had not planned to buy an expensive hat and these hats were expensive, but by then I wanted this extra satisfaction.

The rooms in the millinery department were quiet and exclusive; this was where the richer women took their time in trying on expensive hats. I almost wished now that I had gone back down to the main floor where the hats were cheaper, but it was more dramatic and a bigger point was served by my being in that salon where supposedly the better class of people shopped, away from the hustle and bustle of the street level. I tried to observe the other women on the salon floor out of the corner of my eye, trying to see what their attitudes were. Some left the floor after I came in; others stood in the corner with disgust on their faces, obviously discussing my trying on hats. It was also clear that the salesperson did not really want to serve me but simply had no choice. The feeling of displeasure — if not open hostility — was palpable. I sat there and tried on several hats, even the hats that I knew I would not like. I finally chose one, and they ended up giving it to me, saying they did not want to charge me. They also apologized for the inconvenience and invited me to come again.

In the meantime I noted that the elevator operator, a black woman, kept gazing at me, absolutely awestruck that I was trying on the hats. I was the only black customer and I didn't mention the incident to anybody, but my suspicions were confirmed later on that same evening. The woman elevator operator called a friend of hers, in amazement apparently, to report that a black woman was down in Stewart's trying on hats. Such a thing had never happened before, and the talk about it spread quickly throughout the black community.

As visitors began to come calling on the family at Mr. Clayton's home later that night, my adventure seemed to become the dominant theme of conversation during the grieving hour. Everybody was talking about it. Guess what happened today? It surprised everyone when it turned out that I was the black woman trying on hats at Stewart's.

I found out then that a lot of affluent black women had been shopping at Stewart's for a long time. Black professionals and a lot of middle-class black people certainly had the money to shop there, but the policy was that the store would send the clothes out to the womens' homes. I learned later that stores like Rich's in Atlanta did the same thing.

I know it's hard, especially for younger people, to understand that there could be such controversy over a black woman simply trying on a hat. But in fact, times were tense enough that Ed started to worry about what had happened, afraid there might be some repercussion because I had broken a racial barrier. Charlie Anderson, a prominent Louisville lawyer who had fought many civil rights cases, was planning to come by that evening, so Ed decided he would discuss the incident with him in case there could be any danger in the aftermath. It was actually funny. Charlie started telling Ed about the woman and the hats before Ed had a chance to say anything, and Ed interrupted and said, "Well, I was just going to tell you about that." They had a big laugh about it.

Charlie Anderson told us later that my trying on hats at Stewart's really did break a barrier, that it changed things. It was as if these downtown stores and their managers concluded that nothing spectacular had happened because I tried on hats, nothing disastrous took place, so they changed their policy. It was never tested in any court, never caused a confrontation, but other black women started trying on hats, and then they started trying on shoes and dresses.

I did not do any of this for publicity. If we had pressed it, I think the newspaper and other local media might have run a story, but we were consumed with the funeral, the death of Ed's father. So it never became a news story. I also think now, a long time after the fact, that perhaps the way I handled it had a lot to do with the outcome. I was really hurt when that first saleswoman said to me, "You know you can't try this hat on," and threw the hat down. Her message was clear and so was my outrage, because I was not there trying to lead a demonstration or march around their building. I was there for one purpose, trying to buy a hat for a funeral occasion. My father-in-law had given so much to the community and was held in such high esteem, pictured on the front page of the paper that day, hailed by the local press for being an outstanding citizen, and here a member of his family was not permitted to try on a hat.

I am glad in retrospect that I did not respond with violence or temper or rage, that I went to the executive offices with a degree, I think, of dignity, and told them how I could not believe that such a thing had happened. I think I shamed them into a feeling of guilt. But the fact remains that I never revealed the anger I felt. Or hurt, I should say, because the situation was so absolutely painful.

There is nothing comparable to that kind of pain. If you drop a knife and hit your foot and you cut your toe, of course that hurts. That will hurt you or hurt me, regardless of the color of our skin. But when you are pained in the way I mean, for no explicable reason and for nothing over which you have the least control, that pain is incomparable. I have had all other kinds of pain. I have had cuts and I have been injured and I have been hurt by disappointments. I know that black individuals have suffered much more terrible things, inhuman treatment, but that one personal experience in Louisville still hurts me deeply.

Maybe I was insulated while growing up because of my family and friends, both in Oklahoma and Nashville. Maybe I shouldn't have thought that if you worked hard and got a good education, you would never have to face something like my experience in buying a hat. I had a college degree, money in my pocket, not a lot but adequate funds to afford to buy any hat in that store. I was neatly groomed, but when I walked into that store to buy a hat, I was treated like "just another nigger." It hurts to this day.

The redeeming aspect of the whole experience was that I really did help open another door, help overcome one more barrier. After I got over my immediate hurt, I was able to say, well, something good, after all, came from that. It was what my father often said in his sermons, that something good comes out of every bad situation.

Seven

John H. Johnson, owner of
Johnson Publishing Company and publisher of *Jet* magazine,
had opened a West Coast office, so he asked Ed to move out
to California in 1960. A lot of news for the magazine was
already coming out of Los Angeles. Ed even put out one
special page each week called "The Hollywood Ticker,"
about who was doing what in Hollywood. The magazine had
stringers on the West Coast who were paid to send in items
each week, but there was so much going on, with segregation
barriers starting to crumble and black entertainers opening in
places like the Coconut Grove and the Hollywood Palladium,
that Mr. Johnson felt a need to have a larger presence.

Ed went out first in 1959, and for a while we kept resi-
dences in both Los Angeles and Chicago. We rented a luxury
apartment in a neighborhood called the Wilshire District,
where there were only eleven black people in residence. That
became significant because when Tom Bradley (now mayor of
Los Angeles) first ran for the City Council, he came to us for
assistance, and we were able to drum up quite a bit of support for his campaign. Tom was impressive from the first
time you met him. He had been a career police officer before
getting into politics, and he has proven over the years that he

can put white and black voting coalitions together. He was elected mayor in a city with a hugely white voting majority and later just barely missed being elected governor of California. Sometimes politics ruins people, changes their behavior and their approach to things, but I think Mayor Bradley has always remained a gentleman in the eyes of everybody.

Ed and I landed in Los Angeles with something of a splash because of the national reputation of *Jet* magazine, and we became part of the Los Angeles community right away. The attitude among many black people was that you had really "arrived" if you were mentioned in *Jet*; Ed obviously couldn't put even everyone prominent in the magazine, so it was a special achievement for those who did make it. *Life* and *Newsweek* ran stories about black Americans then, but most publications did not, so *Jet* and *Ebony* were important avenues of exposure. It gave us a badge of identity from the day we arrived in Los Angeles. The magazine did not actually endorse candidates, but Johnson Publications had money and influence, and if you have money or influence, people in politics want to get to know you.

My husband Ed was a dyed-in-the-wool Democrat, as was almost everyone I knew in California (including me), but strangely enough I became an officer in the state *Republican* party.

It was an accident that came about because of another political campaign. I became friends with Jim Flournoy, a black attorney who was running for the State Board of Equalization, which at the time supervised voter registration and election contests. Jim asked me to help him in that campaign, and even though he was a Republican, he was my friend and I wanted to help. As a matter of fact, I ended up running his whole campaign. Frankly, I'm the kind of person likely to give you unsolicited advice, so I started telling Jim he really needed to do this or that, as if I were the great expert. I was hardly an expert and had no great track record of success in political campaigns, but I did have a track record of getting involved and working hard, and I will deliver when I promise something. So I gave Jim advice on everything, including how to dress.

Jim had been active in the Republican party, one of the few blacks who had, and he had certainly paid his dues, so a lot of people in the party felt a responsibility to help him. He got good support, good money coming in for the campaign. Unfortunately, though, his opponent ultimately won the election. But it is worth noting that this was in the early 1960s and Jim got more votes than any black politician ever had in the history of the country. So we felt he had done well even though he lost the race, and he planned to remain active in the party and maybe try again sometime. By this time I had gotten to know all the Republicans who tried to help Jim, had been active at political meetings, and I eventually became a registered Republican.

I met Ronald Reagan at some of those meetings, though not in any significant way because neither of us was particularly important in the party at that time. It was before he became governor and long before he ran for president. I don't know if he would remember me at all, though he might because Jim and I were the only two blacks active in party politics in the state GOP then. Ronald Reagan was well known, of course, because he was Ronald Reagan, but he was only one of many people who had money and power and influence within the party. He came to party meetings like anyone else, but he did not really stand out because there were so many big spenders in the party at that time. In fact, I remember when Reagan ran for governor the first time and I asked my friend Jim about his candidacy. Jim said, "Don't you remember him from all those meetings?"

As a result of getting so involved to help my friend Jim, I ultimately got elected to the State Committee, so I was what you might call a small-time big shot. Jim and I really integrated the Republican party in California. We might have been the only black faces at these meetings, but I suppose even one black face makes you integrated. But I think the GOP party regulars genuinely liked Jim. He didn't browbeat them and he didn't ask for a lot; he was just a nice guy and very religious about showing up for the meetings, paying his dues, and raising money for the party. Whatever moneys they gave to his campaign were probably to ease their guilt for not really cultivating black voters. Jim's extreme loyalty to the party was never really properly rewarded. He deserved much more than he ever received.

•   •   •

It is probably hard for younger people to understand what a special place *Jet* had in the black community at this time, but it was an extremely important source of information about black newsmakers and entertainers. Needless to say, Ed formed a lot of friendships, and black entertainers would often invite him personally to their shows and openings. Our life was much enriched by our show-business friends and connections, and they provided us with many amusing experiences.

There was one hectic, funny day when we entertained friends for dinner, to my great surprise. Ed and I had just been to an opening in Hollywood for Diahnn Carroll, and Lionel Hampton was playing somewhere else the same night. Hampton often played on the West Coast because he had a home there and he enjoyed California, even though he really lived in New York.

As I learned later, Ed had seen Lionel Hampton earlier on this particular day and Hampton had urged him to get some chitterlings to cook that night. Now chitterlings, often called "chitlins," are cooked from the small intestines of pigs. Not everybody likes them, but the people who grew up with them know they can be delicious. Ed was a splendid cook, as his friends knew, and he thought Hampton's suggestion terrific. He told him to come around that evening and that he would also invite some other people. Ed picked up the telephone and invited Diahnn Carroll, Joe Williams, and Billy Eckstine, Nat and Maria Cole, and a lot of others.

I had been out of the house all day and was feeling tired when I got home that evening, thinking that I was going to treat myself to a luxury evening by taking a long hot bath and going to bed early after a bite to eat. I got my bath and put on my bedclothes, and then the doorbell rang and it was June Eckstine. I said something brightly like, "Oh, what a nice surprise." She looked surprised all right and told me that Ed had invited her for dinner, and she was sure other people were coming too. (As an interesting aside, Billy Eckstine was *not* coming. He was married to someone else at this point, and when he learned June would be there, he decided he wouldn't.)

It was not really Ed's fault, let me say, because he had tried to call me and I was not at home. He had planned in any case to get home in plenty of time to give me fair warning, but it turned out that he had trouble finding the chitterlings. Few stores carry them in California, and there are times in the year when they are hard to find anywhere. Then, once Ed finally found some, he had to go somewhere else to find a woman who could clean and cook them. The odor from chitterlings is terribly strong and many people are reluctant to cook them. It is a sure way to let everybody in the neighborhood know what you are going to eat. Ed knew he had invited people over for seven o'clock, and he really was trying to hurry home.

I did not take June Eckstine seriously when she said she had come for dinner. I thought she was really joking and had just dropped by. As far as that goes, I knew we didn't have much food in the house. We kept cheese and snacks, but, with our schedules, we simply did not keep much food at home. We would always go buy special things when we had guests. So I was half-thinking that June must be joking about dinner when the phone rang and it was Diahnn Carrol's agent to tell me that Diahnn was running a little late for dinner but would be along soon.

I phased into panic at this point, not knowing where Ed was nor what these people he invited were supposed to eat for dinner, and by now other people were beginning to arrive. About that time, Lionel Hampton called to ask if Ed had gotten back yet. It seemed that he and Ed had gone together to find the chitterlings, and Ed had promised to come by and pick up Lionel on his way home. That was the first clue I really had as to what was going on.

It was quite a night. We ended up having all these people there for dinner and nothing to feed them, because it takes a long time to cook chitterlings after you clean them, and we figured out they were not going to be ready until late in the night. I was absolutely ready for the divorce court, I was so embarrassed, but all our guests took it in stride, and we sent out for Chinese food. We ended up playing the piano and singing, and everybody — including me — had a good time after all.

My piano saw a lot of musical history. One night Duke Ellington came to our house after an appearance in Los Angeles, and it was as if he were starting his performance all over again, playing the piano until late into the night. He and other entertainers liked to come to our house when they were in Los Angeles, I think, because we were not awed by them, so they could relax and eat and take off their shoes and laugh and talk.

Let me say a friendly word about those chitterlings that got cooked too late in the day to be of much help. Black people relied on them for many years, and consequently they became part of our culture. They are cooked from a part of the pig that white people often threw away, an example of how black folk often had to make use of whatever white folk did not want to eat. We have always had creative ways to survive throughout our history, so we learned to cook chitterlings with such great care that they came to be considered a delicacy. In fact, there was a couple in Los Angeles who had a New Year's Day feast each year, and the hostess always served chitterlings on a silver platter, literally. Friends would breathlessly wait for the coveted invitation to come in the mail. It was one of the grand occasions of the holiday season.

Eight

One of the things I remember about California was working with school dropouts because President John F. Kennedy asked me to do so.

Not quite literally, but it is still true. Late one night I had the radio on, and I happened to hear President Kennedy making a plea for volunteers. It doesn't matter who you are or what your station in life, he said, there is something you can do to make life a little better, and if everybody volunteered, together we could make life better and the community better and the world better. I was already pretty busy, I felt, but President Kennedy sparked my interest. One example he gave of how people might help was with school dropouts, and I knew that our local school dropout rate was high. I served on the board of the Urban League of Los Angeles, and only days before there had been some conversation about the problems at Jordan High School, which was black and Hispanic and had a very high dropout rate.

The school had a gang problem, too, perhaps not like today's when gangs sometimes shoot each other, but still a real concern about rough kids hanging around together, uncontrollable. I almost felt that President Kennedy was talking directly to me when he said you can really achieve something as a volunteer, so the next morning I called Jordan High School. I told them I had heard they already had a program for dropouts, but that I wanted to come by the school and see if there were anything I could do to be of help.

I met with the principal at the school and quickly began to immerse myself in the dropout program. The school was full of Mexicans and blacks, most of them poor, many of whom did not come to school because they were hungry and others who were simply embarrassed that they were so poor. There were also the usual problems—a lack of motivation, a keener interest in mischief than in studies, and a school that in various ways was unable to meet their needs. My thought was that if I could put together a group of volunteers, people willing to give their time, then we could put our efforts together and maybe make a dent in the problem.

I recruited about twenty people who met at my house one evening, friends of mine mostly, professional people who had a lot of energy and a lot of interest in the community. I told them about the dropout program and said, "Let's do something; let's put our heads together and figure out what we can do." They were all eager to try. I called in the school counselor to talk to us in detail about different kinds of problems and options. We decided to take on a hundred dropouts and create relationships with them and in some way try to help get them back in school.

One of my own projects was a young teenager named Barry who was a ringleader among some rough kids. These were tenth and eleventh and twelfth graders, and Barry must have been about sixteen years old. He was a cute little boy, black but with some Hispanic mixed in. He was physically attractive and had the personality of a leader. I got Barry's address and telephone number from the school and went to meet him. I told him who I was and that I wanted to talk to him about some of the problems in school. I said, "Tell you what, Barry, we'll go to lunch and you pick the place; we'll go to the place of your choice." Well, he took me to a drive-in hamburger joint, a dirty place but apparently a hangout for Barry and his friends.

I was dressed like a grown-up married woman, and Barry was dressed like a teenager, not shabby exactly but really casual as high school students tend to be. I pretended that lunch was nothing extraordinary, that I went to run-down diners like that every day. A policeman in the place frowned after we sat down and came over to me and said, "Miss, are you all right?" I said, "Yes, why do you ask?" The police officer nodded at Barry and said, "Because this guy is no good." He said that in Barry's presence.

I had just met Barry but I found myself starting to defend him. What was funny, and I only realized it later, was that Barry had developed a crush on me the minute I came to his home. He wasn't tall, but I am a small woman, so we were about the same height, a couple in size at least. I think he wanted to have lunch at this diner so that people might think I was his girlfriend.

I asked Barry if he belonged to a teenage gang, a group with a particular name who were always meeting and then getting in trouble. He responded that they were a *group*, not a gang, more like a club. I also asked him why he had quit going to school. They weren't teaching him anything, he told me. He said that a lot of his friends didn't go to school either but hung around together instead. I told him that I wanted to come meet with his friends one day.

I could see that threw him some, so I told him there were two things I wanted to do. I wanted to meet with his club or group one day, and I also wanted to meet his parents. That was a must, I decided, because I didn't want his parents to think some strange older woman was trying to lure their son in some bad direction. He finally agreed and said that his mother was home.

When we opened the door, his mother yelled out, "Come on in, boy." His mother was a heavyset, robust woman, and I introduced myself and told her that I was a volunteer in the dropout program, trying to help find out what the problems were with youngsters who dropped out of school. "Somebody sure need to do something," she said, taking up the theme and taking over the conversation. She seemed a strong character and supportive of my involvement, even though she herself had not been able to persuade Barry to stay in school, so we had no problem with her attitude. I told her that from time to time I wanted to meet with Barry because it would be helpful in my work with other children, that although I wanted Barry back in school, I also wanted to help his friends.

Barry's mother seemed to understand my mission, even though I think I was still trying to understand it myself. While I was there, the time came for school to let out, and three other children arrived home, each coming in separately. The first to walk in the door was a boy younger than Barry. The mother never said hello but said something like, "Boy, get in here. I want you to change your clothes and then I want you to wash the dishes," just barking out a list of orders—boom, boom, boom. Then a little girl came in from school, and the mother rattled off orders again, "I want that hair combed, I want you to get your shoes off, and I want you to sweep, and I want you to make up your bed."

I told her I also wanted to meet her husband, just to get more of a feel for the whole family, and I telephoned a few days later to find out when would be a good time. The mother was such a dominant figure that I expected the father to be a small man physically, and, sure enough, he was. Also, as we talked about the school problems with Barry, his answer to any question would be something like, "My wife told me that . . . ."

I didn't let on in that conversation with the father, but the next time I saw Barry I pressed him about his problems and asked why he gave his parents a hard time. He said, without my prompting, that he resented the fact that his father let his mother take over the household and run him.

Was that a plausible explanation for Barry's difficulties? I wasn't any expert, so I went to a psychologist who dealt with children and was told that such a situation often gave children problems. Remember, this was back in the 1960s before women talked quite so much of liberation and the man was the head of the house and the symbol of leadership in the family. I think Barry badly wanted his father to be in charge. He was a respectful little boy and he did not challenge his parents directly, but he deeply resented the fact that his father would not stand up to his mother.

I told Barry again that I still wanted to meet with his group or club. He objected to the word *gang*. It was just a little club, he told me, some kids who liked to get together, and he finally took me to one of their gatherings. There were indeed some rough kids there, some "bad-looking dudes." They had an ongoing contest at that time to see who could steal the most hubcaps. There were a lot of fancy cars around Los Angeles with hubcaps that were specially made, and these kids got a lot of money for them. But the real contest, the challenge, was to see which kid could steal the *most*, and my little boy Barry was always ahead. That was why he was the leader of the group.

I kept trying to persuade Barry that he had ability and that with motivation he could accomplish goals. I told him that was the way people operated in the real world, by setting goals and trying to achieve them, and if he put effort and energy into it, he would reap rewards. I told him that if he put as much energy into his school work as he put into his club and stealing hubcaps, he might end up being President of the United States. I guess because he liked me and trusted me, I began to convince Barry of these things, and he did begin to shape up.

Don't let me leave the impression that all the school dropouts were in gangs and stealing hubcaps. A lot of kids simply did not have any money, and when they wore shabby clothes to school and other kids laughed at them, they would drop out because they could not stand that kind of pressure. Sometimes family problems they couldn't cope with forced kids to stop coming to school. Some were just too ashamed and reticent to ask the teacher about things they did not understand in class, so they would stop coming to school altogether. We found a lot of problems.

The other child besides Barry that I remember best from that time was a young Hispanic girl named Rose. Rose's biggest problem was that there were thirteen children in her family and all of them lived in two bedrooms. Most of the children were girls, so there was a constant scramble for everything in their household. It was a major competition to see who got the toothpaste first, or the hair curlers, or the bathroom. Since there was only one bath, it was often the case that some of the girls wouldn't get a chance to bathe because it would get to be too late at night. The situation affected Rose so that she just could not concentrate at school. Even clothes were a contest. Rose might plan to wear a certain blouse to school and another sister would grab it first. You can understand why she felt so frustrated. She had some drive, but she could not compete with all the other sisters at once.

The other volunteers and I worked with these roughly one hundred children, and we got other people to help us. For the ones who did not have money for clothes, we would go to local merchants and get donations, pants for the boys and skirts and blouses for the girls. We had a regular little clothing supply operation working, and we managed to get some kids back in school just by outfitting them with clothes. We also bought books and pencils and notebooks for the students who could not afford school supplies. Other problems, as with Barry, were a matter of getting the student motivated to go back to school or, in many cases, getting the teachers to agree to take these youngsters back. We found many teachers who felt that they simply didn't have time to try again with the kids who had dropped out or been dismissed. So we developed a working agreement with the school to the effect that if we could get kids back to school, the school would agree to put them back in the same grade level. Then we would try to help motivate them.

Some eighty-one of those roughly one hundred dropouts went back to school and graduated. We thought that was a mighty good success rate.

I said earlier that I got started in this volunteer dropout program because of hearing President Kennedy urge volunteers to make a difference and feeling almost that he was talking to me. You can imagine what a thrill it was when we got a message from the White House that they had heard about our dropout volunteer program in Los Angeles and President Kennedy himself was going to present the program with a special award. I was invited to the White House to help accept the honor, and everybody at the school was very excited.

But it was not to be. We were to go to the White House in December of 1963. President Kennedy was murdered in Dallas in late November, only a few days earlier. The award ceremony never took place, but we were proud just the same. We grieved for President Kennedy, but even that did not dampen the success of the project. Barry was one of the kids who went back to school and stayed and graduated. So was Rose. I like to think that President Kennedy would have been proud of them.

The great memories of my life relate to helping children, perhaps because of my own personal experience. In the early years of my marriage I expected, like almost everybody else, to have a family. I made every effort to have children and was pronounced healthy by my physical exams. Ed and I both had such a strong love for children and were so looking forward to our own family that I went through an awful time during the first phase of my marriage, psychologically, because I could not understand why I could not have children.

My religious faith was strong, of course, and my friends kept saying, "Oh, the Lord will answer your prayers to have a family." I prayed and prayed and prayed and prayed, and every time I would talk to a minister I would say, "Now listen, I think something is wrong with God, because here I am with my love for children, and my husband and I can afford them financially and I am healthy and strong." I would read about children being neglected and think, how can this happen when I would love and take such good care of my own children?

Then one minister said to me that maybe the Lord had a different purpose for me. I thought at first that that seemed far-fetched. What an answer from a minister, I thought, since what better mission could the Lord have for me than to have children and nurture them and give them understanding and love? It was not until I began working with the dropout program that I realized this must be the mission the Lord had given me. If I had had my own children, from what I can understand from parents, it would have been hard to even think about helping other people's children. As it was, I was able to devote all my energy to this project, and perhaps I helped save eighty children where otherwise I might have been caring for only one or two.

Barry and Rose ended up staying in high school and graduating. Rose went on to a state college because I was able to help her get a scholarship. She still had almost no money, and I was going to drive her to the college on her first day on campus. Suddenly, on the day before we were to leave, I realized she did not have the essentials; she didn't even have a suitcase. So I drove by and picked her up and we got a suitcase; then we went to a drugstore and bought about one hundred dollars worth of cosmetics and other basics that she would need away at school. I still remember how much fun it was to be Mom for the day.

Rose had been in college for two or three months when I got another chance. She called to ask if I would come be her Mom for Mother's Day. I told her I would be delighted. Most of the students were white, and they had a kind of shocked reaction to see this black woman as Rose's mom. But the students were all nice. Rose had some wonderful friends, and I was so honored to be Rose's mom that day. Her own mother did not speak English and was probably, well, not uninterested but not comfortable at the thought of coming to Mother's Day. Also, they were such a poor family that Rose may have felt her mother could not afford to come.

I know this — she really wanted me to come, and I know how much I enjoyed being there with her.

Nine

It was a hard decision for us to leave California so that Ed could come to work for Dr. King and the Southern Christian Leadership Conference.

Neither of us really knew Dr. King personally. I had met him when I attended church conventions where he was a speaker, long before he became so nationally famous, and I knew he was an eloquent speaker. Ed had never met him in person, but his reporters had covered King and the civil rights movement, so he knew a lot about him. But Ed was already highly respected for his role at *Jet* magazine, he was earning a good salary from Johnson Publishing, and really he was at the peak of his career with no immediate interest in making a change.

Yet it was hard to say no to Dr. King.

Dr. King was feeling the increased wear and tear of his organizational efforts. He badly needed an experienced journalist who could help with public relations and the media, with speechwriting and press releases. He would mention this to people he met traveling around the country, telling them how he really needed a strong public relations person, and he got the same answer over and over: the person you really need, even though you probably can't get him, is Ed Clayton.

He would be the best man for the job. Dr. King decided to call Ed and try to talk him into coming to Atlanta.

Ed was reluctant to leave *Jet*, but he was also reluctant to say no, recognizing the significance of the work Dr. King was doing and feeling that it was maybe now his duty to make this sacrifice. He knew the SCLC couldn't pay him nearly as much money as he was making, but that was not a big factor. So after talking with Martin at length, Ed decided to take a three-month leave to come to Atlanta to set up an improved public relations system for the SCLC.

I stayed in California and Ed moved on to Atlanta for three months. He began to help Martin write speeches and compile materials and get press packets together and plan press conferences and do all the kinds of things good public relations people do, and indeed he was able to help ease Dr. King's burdens. But the three months went by too quickly, and since Dr. King thought Ed had done a splendid job, he said to Ed, "I need you. Will you give me another three months?" This was in early 1963, getting close to the final planning for that year's March on Washington, and Dr. King felt that event was so important that it was hard for Ed to say anything but yes to the second three months.

It was about that time that I started traveling with Coretta King. Ed had talked with her and found that she had a real yearning to be more active in fundraising, and Ed suggested that her professional singing ability might be the way. Coretta said that she would love to do some concerts if they could raise money for the SCLC, and Ed urged her to let him help her set it up. So they talked about the mechanics of it, and Ed put together a press kit and got pictures made and they began scheduling tours. Somewhere in there he told Coretta that I would be a good person to travel with her, because I had great organizational ability. The Kings did not know much about me then, but Ed had told them I was a musician and could handle travel plans and any other details that needed to be handled.

The decision was made to launch the Freedom Concert Tour on the West Coast in view of the strong support of the Western Christian Leadership Conference. The WCLC was the western affiliate of the SCLC and was comprised, chiefly, of ministers who were consistently loyal to and supportive of Dr. King and his movement. The organization included such outstanding clergy as Dr. Thomas Kilgore, Bishop H. H. Brookins, Dr. E. V. Hill, Dr. Maurice Dawkins, Rev. Mansfield Collins, Dr. Marvin Robinson, Rev. A. A. Peters, and Rev. Larry Odom. So Ed and I planned the tour from Los Angeles, and I met Coretta when she flew in and became her traveling companion. The first concert was in Los Angeles, followed by San Diego, Seattle, Portland, and San Francisco. Coretta seemed pleased with everything I did.

There were some moments of strain, and Coretta always seemed to think first of the people with her. After the program in Seattle, we were all taken to the home of a woman who supposedly was going to offer us dinner. After we arrived, she asked Coretta how she wanted her steak cooked, and Coretta indicated her preference. Then, a little later when the steak came, the rest of us—two security persons, two musicians, and I—were offered cold cuts and potato salad. It was embarrassing for Coretta because she could not imagine eating steak while the rest of us had cold plates. So she turned the steak down, which offended the hostess. None of us ate anything at that house, but we all had a good meal together when we got back to the hotel.

Coretta was the gracious lady, always, and I was the lady charged with keeping us to the schedule. I was the one who would bring the press conference to an end, even when some reporters still wanted to ask questions, and I think Coretta liked the way I handled those difficult chores. No matter how well you plan things, you never can tell what is going to come up unexpectedly, and the unexpected things were the things I handled best. When we got back to Atlanta, Coretta was full of praise for the way I had helped her on the concert tour.

The March on Washington in 1963 was widely considered the emotional and even intellectual high point of the civil rights movement. It captured the attention of millions across the nation, not only those on the scene to hear Dr. King's "I Have a Dream" speech. It lent momentum to the drive for the civil rights legislation that would be passed by Congress in 1964 and 1965. Ed was very much a part of the writing of that great speech, and to me this still means that Ed played a wonderful role in something that is history. He would write a section of the speech and Dr. King would edit it, and they would worry it back and forth. Dr. King wanted it to be just right. When Ed drafted something good, Dr. King would say it was good. Then he would say he wanted to add this and that, and they went back and forth on that speech. It was just wonderful.

Ed contributed a lot to the speech, but let me note that that great section near the end, the words everyone remembers, "I have a dream," and then the rest about the sons and daughters of slaves and of slave owners sitting down together in his own state of Georgia, that was all pure Dr. King, the words springing from his character and soul. Still, Ed contributed significantly to the overall content of this and other speeches, and he was proud to be able to make such a contribution.

Ed really was very good at the things he did for the SCLC. He brought a high level of creativity to the work and a verve and enthusiasm that affected others on the staff. They put together a souvenir journal to help raise money, a journal that documented the history of the SCLC, and Ed started newsletters to send out to the SCLC affiliates all around the country. Dr. King especially liked building that connection between the people in the local affiliates and the home office, letting them know exactly what he and the Rev. Ralph David Abernathy were doing. Ed would also send out copies of Dr. King's speeches and design fundraising materials to send to supporters around the country. So he helped generate funds, and he put a high polish on the public relations image of the organization, gave it a first class presentation, all of which was greatly appreciated by the board of the SCLC and by Dr. King personally.

So Ed's first three months were extended to another three months, and by this time both Dr. King and Coretta began to put pressure on me to move permanently from California to Atlanta. But really I had no intention at all of moving to Atlanta. I had come to Atlanta to visit, and the truth is, at that time I really did not like Atlanta.

Segregation was still in place, but that wasn't a big problem for us. The community where Ed and I ultimately chose to live was a black middle-class community. We worked on Auburn Avenue and lived in the southwest part of Atlanta, mostly black, so there was no obvious segregation barrier to overcome, and some of the barriers were already falling, even before the civil rights legislation passed. I remember Macy's, or Davison's then, had just opened its Tea Room, and Coretta took me down there for lunch and also to the Magnolia Room at Rich's. So there were some nice places for me to go, already integrated at that time.

Dr. King used to tease me about not marching with him, but there was one time I marched with Coretta, soon after moving to Atlanta. Thompson Boland Lee was a popular shoe store with quality merchandise, so women wanted to shop there and men wanted to work there. The store didn't mind taking black women's money, but they had only white salesmen, even though we knew that experienced black salespersons had applied and been turned down. The store refused to let black men work there because of that old attitude that a black man looking up a white woman's dress was absolutely unthinkable.

Coretta put together a group of black women who could well afford to buy their shoes at this store, and she decided we would have our own protest. We would simply say we were not going to shop there anymore unless the store hired some black salesmen, and we marched for two days in front of the store. Our two-day march and other negotiations led the store to change its policy and hire some black salesmen.

But back to my reluctance to move to Atlanta from California. It was not that I had any fear of moving to the Deep South or concern about segregation. Frankly, this was just before Atlanta emerged as a truly major city, and at that time I had the impression that everything in Atlanta closed up at nine-thirty at night. I was something of a night person at the time, and in Los Angeles you could go out to the laundromat at midnight or go for a hamburger at three in the morning or get up if you had insomnia and go *somewhere*. Los Angeles was a twenty-four hour town, and while wandering around at three in the morning wasn't the biggest thing in life for me, the idea that there wasn't anywhere to go late at night in Atlanta was less than appealing when I thought about moving.

Atlanta was also a much smaller town than Los Angeles. The expressway even to the airport was unfinished. I remember you had to get off at the end of the expressway and go through the small town of Hapeville, and you had to cross a railroad track where there always seemed to be forty miles of train blocking your way if you were in a hurry. Most black middle-class families lived in southwest Atlanta, and the expressway towards that side of the city ended at Hunter. You had to get off there and cut over to Hightower Road to get to the rest of the community, and some of the streets were not even paved. So there was all that red Georgia clay I had heard about. In short, I didn't find Atlanta the glamorous place that many praised in such high terms, and I was very reluctant to move.

But there was a lot of coaxing. Dr. King kept making me offers. He promised me a decent job with a good salary, and he said he would help us find a house. After a lot of entreaty I finally moved, and he paid me, of course, what the SCLC budget could afford. I used to tease him—"Where is that big salary you were going to pay me?"

Ed had to resign from Johnson Publishing if he were going to work on with Dr. King, and I know he felt he was making a sacrifice. I suppose I felt the same in moving from California, but neither of us ever regretted it. Ed died so unexpectedly, in 1966, but those last three years of his life with Dr. King were part of history. He made his contribution.

Ten

People have often asked me what it was like growing up as an identical twin, half of a dual life. The fact is that it has always affected everything in my life, including the time when Ed and I were courting and then about to get married. My sister and I have told people, sometimes, that we don't quite know what it would be like *not* to have this dual life since that is all we have ever known.

What was wonderful about our lives growing up as twins was that we never had any sense of competition. One twin typically, I have read, tends to be the dominant one, and that was true in our case. We were born ten minutes apart, and I am the older. I don't know if that's the reason, but I was always the slightly dominant one, and my sister seemed to be happy to follow my lead. I always had this strong sense that I *wanted* to lead, and my sister seemed comfortable following that lead, so we were never in competition and always had a loving relationship.

Psychologists have written that this pattern is often typical of twins. Our only problems came from outside intervention. Somebody might say to my sister, talking about me, "Are you going to let her tell you what to do? Don't you have a mind of your own?" This would get my sister stirred up for a minute, but we were so close that usually she would still end up listening to me. In everyday life this pattern worked fine. I decided what we would wear and how we would do our hair and whether we would go here or there or yon. Sometimes I would just plant the seed, not really give orders, and my sister would almost always follow my lead. The one great exception was when it came to romance. We found that something happened there which was really interesting.

My sister was much more active as a youngster than I and much more gregarious. She liked boys first, she tried cigarettes first, and she was generally more experimental. I was the dominant one of our twindom, but I was a little reluctant to be exploratory or rebellious. I think I just always wanted to operate by the rules. My twin, though, didn't feel quite so constrained. Her zest for living gave joy to almost everyone around her.

We would move around the school when we were teenagers, the way girls will do, setting our eye on this boy or that. I would support my sister theoretically and philosophically and encourage her if she found a cute boy and wanted to make her play for him, but then if it worked out, I immediately hated the guy. This was not so serious when we were going through the puppy-love stage in high school, but when we got to college where any romance might lead to marriage, it became more serious. So every time my sister got a boyfriend, I would like him up to the point that she decided she *really* liked him, and then I hated him. She reacted the same way with my boyfriends, but since she had more boyfriends than I did, I ended up hating more boys.

However, neither of us got married while in college, and after we moved to Chicago together, it turned out that I got married first. My sister liked Ed; as a matter of fact, at first she pushed me faster than I was ready to go. I was not at all sure at first that I loved him, but my sister kept saying things like, "Oh, it would be wonderful to have him in the family; I would love to have him as a brother-in-law." Of course, when

Ed and I did finally fall in love and start planning on marriage, she did a complete about-face.

Suddenly she didn't like Ed at all, and it showed in different ways. Naturally, we planned for my sister to stand up with me at the wedding, and while we shopped together for my wedding dress, she was also supposed to be looking for the proper dress for herself. I don't know how men are, but with women it always seems that we can never find what we want when we want it. If we go out shopping for a specific garment, that is often exactly what we can't find. We had started our wedding-day shopping well in advance, and as we shopped for other things I constantly urged her to look for the dress she would need. Well, she would put me off, saying she would do it tomorrow. That's all I heard—tomorrow and tomorrow and tomorrow. The truth was that she was hedging; she didn't want to buy the dress because she didn't want to be in the wedding because she simply didn't want there even to *be* a wedding.

But to back up a bit, Ed was very perceptive about this jealousy between my sister and me. He was keenly sensitive to our closeness, and he played it very safely and successfully. He did not make the mistake of trying to separate us; rather he tried to combine us. He was invited to a lot of openings, nightclubs and whatever, and he would call me often before we were married and ask me to get dressed so that we could go out, maybe to a Nat King Cole opening. Then he would add that he would like it if Little—that's my sister's nickname—could join us.

Although my sister and I are identical twins, there was one slight difference: my face was a little bit rounder. It was not a great difference, but our friends could tell, so when we were girls they started calling me "Big" and my sister "Little." It may be also that those nicknames were a little easier to handle than our given names, Xernona and Xenobia.

At any rate, Ed would always try to include Little when we went out. It got to be a running joke because Ed was well known around Chicago and would often be introduced at places or events. Sometimes the introduction would be, "Well, we're glad to have Ed Clayton here tonight and his twin wives." Another joke about it stemmed from the fact that I did not drink at all and my sister did. Ed would say that he needed to bring my sister along so that she could help use up the two-drink minimum; it was just not cost effective to take me out alone.

On my first birthday while we were courting Ed gave me an expensive watch for my present and he took me out to dinner. He invited Little along and — guess what? — he had bought her an identical watch for *her* birthday present. The first Christmas after we were married Ed bought me a beautiful fox-trimmed coat. He got me to come down to the store after he had picked it out, just to be sure I liked it before we actually took it home, and I learned from the saleslady that he had bought two identical coats. He helped us keep that twin feeling and I loved that he wanted to keep us together. I didn't feel that I had run out on my sister, and she didn't feel that she had to hate him.

This may sound crazy, but my sister even came along with us on our honeymoon. It was at Ed's request. We planned a trip to New York, and she accepted Ed's invitation, and we all enjoyed her being there. I guess I should say that we didn't all stay in the same hotel room.

My sister did not get married until a long time after I did, and in the meantime she became ill with multiple sclerosis. She had been working full-time, living alone now in the apartment we had shared before my marriage, and she was ill so long that she used up all her health insurance benefits and was still bedridden when she was released from the hospital. That meant she needed full-time care. She could have moved in with us, but that would have destroyed her independence, and her doctor told us that that was a delicate concern for someone who had been so ill. It turned out that we had a friend, Connye Hornsby, not working at the time, who already knew my sister and whom my sister trusted, so we hired her to take care of Little. It was Ed who insisted on paying for this full-time care.

Little did get better and got married, but you don't recover from multiple sclerosis; it just gets worse. My sister sometimes feels good, but no two days are alike. She has difficulty moving around but maintains a beautiful, cheerful, and happy attitude, and she's great fun to be around. A motorized scooter helps her navigate around, a gift from our brother James and his wife Thelma.

When Little decided to marry Tony Smith, I objected vehemently. The stress of her illness and my behavior weighed on her heavily, and I relented and reluctantly gave her my blessings. I subsequently regretted my initial disapproval of Tony, for he turned out to be a wonderful mate. He loved my sister, nursed her during her immobile days, anticipated and met her every need. He proved to be a reliable and responsible husband and father. They are still together after nearly thirty years of marriage.

People have asked me if any of these strange stories could be true about the unusual experiences that twins are reported to have. I know of one from my own life. Little met her husband-to-be when she came to visit us in California, and after her marriage she defied medical science by insisting that she wanted to have a baby. Her doctors advised her strongly against it, telling her that because of her health either she would not be able to carry the baby to full term or, perhaps worse, the baby might be born with some serious abnormality. "I understand the risks," she told her doctors, "but let me go as far as I can, and we will see what happens in the end." Well, the child was born, and it was in fact abnormal, but not in the way doctors had feared. The young boy, Bradford, was such a totally healthy child that he never had a cold until he was four years old. He never cried, he slept all night, and he was a wonderful baby in every way.

Here is where the story gets odd.

My sister's child was born on June 21, 1966, while she was in California and I was in Atlanta. Actually, her pregnancy had turned out to be an easy one despite the worry of the doctors. She had no morning sickness nor any labor pains, right up to the moment when she went to the hospital. I had telephoned her that day just to see if there were any news, and she said she was feeling fine but nothing was happening yet as far as she could make out. She said she had no idea when she might need to go to the hospital.

Don't forget the three-hour difference between Atlanta time and the West Coast time. Some friends of ours, Dr. Roy Bell and his wife, dropped by our home about six that evening. We were getting ready to fix something to eat and asked them to stay. They tried to decline, but we insisted, and even though we had barely enough food for all of us, we ended up having a good time, sitting at the kitchen table and talking away.

It was a quarter to twelve Atlanta time. I can remember that exactly because Dr. Bell called attention to it, saying something jokingly, like, "Fine friends we are. We say we are going to drop by for a few minutes, and here we are still sitting here at almost midnight." No more than a minute later this terrible pain hit me, just nearly killed me, a pain that seemed to start at my left shoulder and cross my body and run down to my right thigh. It left me almost breathless, and I even cried out from it.

We were all concerned, but Dr. Bell figured that it was probably a cramp pain, maybe from something I ate or from sitting in the same position for several hours. Anyway, the pain passed and I got my breath back and was all right.

My brother-in-law called me the first thing the next morning and told me that he had taken my sister to the hospital the night before to have her baby. He even said, "You know how she never had a pain during pregnancy? Well, she finally had a pretty good one last night." It was near her due date, so Little's husband was watching over her pretty closely. He told me that he asked her about 8:30 p.m. when she was going to bed, and she said pretty soon. She was still piddling around at a quarter to nine, and that was when her pain struck—a terrible labor pain that went from her right side across her body to her left leg. Now, I didn't tell my brother-in-law that anything had happened to me, but I did ask him to tell me again how he could be sure the pain hit at quarter to nine and to describe the pain again.

It was true. My sister's first severe labor pain in California came at exactly the same time my pain hit me in my kitchen in Atlanta, and it was as if the two pains were mirror images, hers from the right shoulder diagonally across her body to her left leg and mine from the left shoulder down to my right leg. I can't explain it. But my husband and Dr. Bell and his wife were with me when I had that sudden terrible pain at quarter to twelve, and I had no way in the world of knowing that my sister was suffering her first hard labor pain at exactly the same time in California, three thousand miles away. They were there to confirm my story, so no one can accuse me of imagining things, even though this was something just too bizarre to be believable.

There is something eerie in the special chemistry between twins. I can't explain it, but I can vouch for it. It's wonderful.

The Brewster twins read about themselves in the paper (Xernona, left, and Xenobia).

Xernona's sister Xenobia, U.S. Congressman Louis Stokes, Xernona, and Dorothea Williams, with Xernona's five-year-old nephew Bradford.

Family photo: brother James Brewster and his wife Thelma; brother-in-law Tony Smith and Xenobia with their son Bradford; Xernona and husband Paul Brady.

Coretta Scott King and Xernona.

Atlanta journalist Paulyne Morgan White, Julie Belafonte, Harry Belafonte, and Xernona in Jamaica.

Xernona with Harry Belafonte and Sidney Poitier.

Former Georgia labor commissioner Sam Caldwell and Xernona.

California senator Diane Watson, Xernona, Lillian Lewis, Jo Bridges, and senator Sonjia Young.

Chicago journalist Mattie Smith Colin, Xernona, and Rosa Parks.

Xernona and Virginia governor Douglas Wilder, former Atlanta mayor Andrew Young, and SCLC president Rev. Joseph Lowery.

Leroy Johnson, Georgia's first black senator, and Xernona welcomed at the State Capitol by the governor Lester Maddox of Georgia.

Xernona interviews Lena Horne.

Xernona hugged by Oprah Winfrey; looking on are Donald C. Walker, publisher of Dollars & Sense *magazine, Etta Moten (hidden), and Rev. Addie Wyatt.*

Xernona interviews Carol Channing.

Annual Christmas party on the set of "The Xernona Clayton Show."

Mrs. Ralph McGill (Dr. Mary Lynn Morgan) and Xernona.

Eleven

No one knew it would be Dr. King's last birthday, of course, but there were other reasons why we tried to make that last January celebration something special.

Dr. King had voiced his strong opposition to the war in Vietnam, and it hurt him that he received so much criticism from friends who had always supported him in the past. He seemed so low in spirit during those days. I remember it was Andy Young and Ralph Abernathy, undoubtedly his closest friends on the SCLC staff, who started saying that we had to do something special, something just to "cheer Doc up."

The SCLC staff had always given Dr. King a new black suit on his birthday, so that gift was pretty well established. He liked a formal black suit when he spoke—his uniform, more or less—and he made so many public appearances that he always wore those suits out by the time his birthday rolled around. So the staff would chip in to buy him a good suit every year, but this year we wanted to do something different, too.

His executive staff was in Atlanta for a meeting that January 15, all down at Ebenezer Church for a planning session. Andy Young called me at home and told me that he and

Ralph Abernathy had just been talking about how down Doc
had been—almost everyone on the staff called Dr. King
"Doc"—and we really ought to try to cheer him up, somehow make it a special birthday, a fun time.

It was already about two in the afternoon and I tried to
escape the task, telling Andy that I was just not good on the
spur of the moment, that I needed time to think and plan for
such a thing. Andy insisted, "Oh, you can do it," he said, and
told me he would expect to see me at the church at five
o'clock. They already had a big birthday cake, and they
would start the celebration when I got there.

I hung up the telephone and tried to think what in the
world I could do in just a couple of hours. I was in the house
by myself, and nothing there gave me any inspiration, but just
as I was leaving, I noticed this gold cup on my dresser. It was
like the tin cups you used to see in Western movies, except
gold, and I took it along hoping I might do something clever
with it.

At the church we had the cake, and we joked and tried to
make Dr. King smile. I presented him with my gold cup and
made a little speech to go with it. I told Dr. King that we had
all worried about how to honor him on this particular birthday, and I also knew how hard he had worked trying to help
in President Johnson's War on Poverty. "So here's something
you can do," I told him, and I handed him the gold cup.
"You can stand on the downtown street corners and take up
collections to help fight the War on Poverty." Oh, it may
sound silly, but Dr. King was delighted; he laughed and
laughed. He kept on laughing when I added that, incidentally,
I wanted my cup back sometime because after all it was *my
only* gold cup.

It was a coincidental thing, but that birthday celebration in
Ebenezer got filmed by an Italian television crew following
Dr. King around, filming footage for part of a documentary,
and that film has since been seen by a great many people.
CNN runs it every year in January during the week of King's

birthday holiday, and it has also been included in other network television shows. *Time* magazine once wrote that Dr.
King had no sense of humor, I suppose because their
reporters always saw him in more formal settings when
humor was not appropriate, but he did have a great sense of
humor. I pretended that I was trying to take my gold cup
back, and he laughed so hard he almost fell back into his
chair. I think people like that film because it does show a side
of Martin that many never had a chance to see. As a matter
of fact, when Coretta King was asked to be technical adviser
on the movie *From Montgomery to Memphis*, she recommended they include this film footage both because it was
Martin's last birthday and also because it was one of the few
times the public would be able to see him laughing.

Those moments of laughter that day were important to
Martin and to his friends because we had not seen him laugh
much for a while, and that was why Rev. Young and Rev.
Abernathy were so anxious to have something special on that
birthday.

The criticism of his stand on Vietnam greatly affected his
mood, and you could tell when you talked to him that he was
clearly pained and disappointed. I don't want to say
depressed because that sounds like a psychotic state, but he
was certainly very emotionally down and emotionally
drained at this point. He felt that the mood of the country
had swung away from his values to the extent that maybe *he*
was the misfit. He worried that programs he believed important could not be implemented, given the mood of the country. He talked so poignantly, sadly about the many old
friends who were telling him that he was wrong to speak out
on Vietnam. He felt for the first time that he was out there
marching by himself, without the wealth of friends and supporters who had been with him in the past.

It was April 4, 1967, when Dr. King broke his silence on
Vietnam in a sermon at Riverside Church in New York. In
harsh language, he accused the government of diverting

funds from the poverty program to fuel the Asian war and of cruelly manipulating young black men and women by sending them thousands of miles away to help assure liberties in Southeast Asia which they could not find in Southwest Atlanta . . . Northeast Alabama . . . nor Northwest Chicago. Dr. King described President Johnson's administration as the "greatest purveyor of violence in the world today."

This speech immediately diminished support for Dr. King. His denunciation of the Vietnam War caused many to withdraw and separate themselves from his movement. This defection of his friends, both black and white, made Dr. King feel isolated, seemingly the "sole voice" of anti-war sentiment. Exhausted yet strongly committed, he persevered. He never changed his moral consciousness about peace . . . and I believe history is on his side.

I will always remember with a happy feeling how special that celebration of Martin's last birthday was and, also, what a good time we had at his house on the Sunday not long before that last trip to Memphis. Both his mother and I played the piano, with the family all singing and joking.

He was somber on that ride out to the Atlanta airport just before he was killed, worried that people had infiltrated the last march in Memphis in order deliberately to cause violence and concerned that there might be more violence. But he was cheerful, too, talking about our singing session that Sunday and how much fun that had been. I told him that his mother had called me later to say the same thing. She had told me that she knew how busy Martin was, with everybody pulling at him, but that the first chance I got she wanted me to speak up for her and tell him how much she had enjoyed being with him on Sunday and how much she wanted to spend more time with her son, even if only on the telephone.

Martin was in better spirits by the time we got to the airport, and he was teasing me again about how I never marched with him. I told him, "That's because they always throw you in jail and you have to have somebody outside to raise your bail money." We were running late as we got to the airport, almost flight time, and asked which gate he needed. It was almost the furthest concourse away, which made us laugh again. Martin made a joke of it and insisted I leave the car right there on the curb and race with him to reach the gate.

"You've never marched," he said, "so let me see you do this. Maybe if you run down to the gate with me I'll consider that you have marched; we'll just make this your march." He grabbed my arm and half dragged me along as we raced to make his plane. It was hardly a march since we ran all the way to the gate and were both out of breath when we got there. But he was still in great humor as he realized he would make the plane on time. "Well, I got you to do something I never thought I would get a chance to do," he said, "make at least a semblance of a march."

That was the last time I saw him.

The week after Martin's funeral, as things were beginning to settle down a little bit, I spent a lot of time at his mother's house trying to help her with answering telephones and letters and keeping her company. She told me that Martin had telephoned her from Memphis on his last day on earth, and they had talked for more than an hour. It was a sad time, but she was so joyful about that, that she at least had talked to her son for a long while on his last day. She thanked me for reminding him to call.

Twelve

I was teasing Dr. King when I offered him that gold cup so that he would stand on street corners and beg for money to help in the War on Poverty, but only three weeks later I myself signed on in that war.

The director of the Model Cities program in Atlanta, Johnny Johnson, asked me to become community affairs coordinator for the program, and I saw it as an exciting opportunity. Model Cities was the federal government's most determined effort up until that time to try to deal with the problems of the poor. There were some failures, but also some great successes that came from the program.

Some stories from the Model Cities effort even had a certain humorous side. I spent a lot of time visiting with people in public housing projects since Model Cities was trying to encourage poor people in every possible way, urging youngsters to stay in school, finding jobs, even in some cases subsidizing low-cost housing outside the projects. There was some grumbling about me because I dressed each day in what some considered too high a style to be appropriate for visiting with the disadvantaged. I merely considered it professional attire. Now, I had always tried to dress appropriately, and in this period in my life I wore white gloves every day and I fixed my hair in an upswept hairdo with a head band. I do not think my white gloves or my hair or my clothes were in any way overly elaborate, but some critics complained that anyone who wore white gloves and dressed in that fashion could not possibly relate to underprivileged people.

Women living in the projects quickly came to my defense. They told members of the City Council that their children, especially the young girls, were thrilled when I came to visit them. The girls told their mothers how they wanted to look like me when they grew up, to dress well and wear white gloves. They saw me as a role model, I suppose, and I certainly tried to encourage those young girls to want to make something of themselves.

I also got along well with many of the young teenage boys on the streets. Some were frightening at first encounter, guys who carried guns and knives, but I tried to talk to them in a reaching-out manner, and we usually made friends. There was one group of dozens of such young men who hung around together in a parking lot near a liquor store. They had nicknames like Two Gun Pete, Malt Liquor, and Stumpy Joe, but I liked them and teased them about how they really ought to get jobs.

"Jobs?" they would ask incredulously. They would insist that they were not the kind of people anybody wanted to hire; most were school dropouts, and many had police records. I finally said to this whole big group of young men one fine day that I felt sure I could find them jobs if they were willing to work. They took this as a challenge, and so did I.

The next thing I did was to pay a visit to Sam Caldwell, then the state commissioner of labor. I told Commissioner Caldwell that there was no funding in the Model Cities program for jobs for such dropouts but that, surely, there must be some state program that would give them a chance. Commissioner Caldwell was cautious, but said he would be willing to discuss the matter with the young men. But he warned me that any jobs would probably be minimum wage work that required no training, like cleaning the streets.

Many of the young men who gathered in that parking lot were teenagers, but some of the leaders were older, young men in their twenties who had made a life on the streets.

John "Malt Liquor" Patrick, for instance, was in his late-twenties, a great big hulking man, over six-feet-three and weighing close to 250 pounds. He was one of six children, born in a poor neighborhood, Summerhill, and by the time he was a teenager he was hanging around on street corners. By age seventeen he was on his way to jail, for assorted cases of stabbing people on the street. "I came to the corner young," he told one journalist after I had gotten him involved in helping find jobs for supposedly unemployable ghetto youths. "That's what gets a kid. I'd be hanging around with these older fellas and they'd say, 'You won't cut him,' and I'd say, 'Yeah, I will,' and I'd go grab a man and cut him up. It was just a dare but I'd do it. My mother would talk to me and I'd listen, but then I'd go back to the corner and it would be the same thing. It cost me seven and a half years in jail. I thought I was being smart, but I found out I was being a fool."

Some of the tougher guys in my street corner gang, like Malt Liquor, found it hard to believe that the labor commissioner of the state of Georgia would be willing to help find them jobs. I urged them to select four or five leaders from their group to go with me to visit Commissioner Caldwell in his office, but they were still doubtful. Finally they declared that if the state labor commissioner really wanted to talk to them about jobs, then he ought to come down to their street corner and talk there. I tried to persuade them that this was crazy and unreasonable, without success, so I then found myself returning a bit hesitantly to Commissioner Caldwell's office to ask him if he would meet with these young men in the streets, their own territory. He laughed considerably at the idea, but he said he would do it. He met with them and, being assured they were serious, promised to find jobs for them.

That was the beginning of a program that eventually put hundreds of young men into city maintenance jobs. A lot of them worked hard and seemed grateful for the chance; others in the group quickly vanished at the prospect of actually going to work.

The Model Cities program created some curious contacts for me. As coordinator, I sometimes conducted biracial neighborhood meetings, and one took place in a largely white neighborhood, the Adair area of Atlanta. I had been told that the Georgia Grand Dragon of the Ku Klux Klan, Calvin Craig, lived in that neighborhood and indeed that he had become chairman of the Model Cities program for the Adair Park neighborhood, but I had never met him before our Model Cities meeting at a community center one September night. He was a tall, well-dressed, and attractive man with a pleasant smile, and he carried himself with a curious, elastic grace. He was the sort of polite, soft-voiced man I might have mistaken for a business executive, rather than a leader of a group who wore white robes and burned crosses as part of their expression of racial hate.

I did not recognize him when I first met him at the meeting, though I received one immediate clue. He was standing to the left of the door when I arrived at the center, talking to two other men, both of whom came forward and greeted me with warm handshakes. This man approached me reluctantly, offering a stinting four fingertips as a handshake. Liberal white friends had told me that this gesture was a sure sign of a bigot.

But I still had no real indication of who he was, even though there were soon some other clues. Other participants began to gather, and the crowd grew larger. One black man sat down beside Calvin Craig, and he promptly moved elsewhere. He had not been seated in his new location very long before a black woman sat down beside him. He moved again.

Now I began to think there really was something behind the fingertips-only handshake. Yet it was my duty as program coordinator to relate to all people in the six communities of the Model Cities district, some of them predominantly black, some mostly white. Even so, by the time the meeting was over I understood that this Mr. Calvin Craig was the Grand Dragon of the Ku Klux Klan, and his actions clearly indicated his dislike of black people.

The Grand Dragon came by my office on a Monday not long after that meeting to talk about some aspects of the Model Cities program and why he felt they might not work in Adair Park. I felt at once on the defensive, fearful of anyone with a Ku Klux Klan connection, but I tried to mask my apprehension and answer his questions with kindness and civility. After all, I told myself, here is a human being who needs help. I did not seek directly to try to change his views. I thought I should listen carefully to him first, and many things he said to me revealed that he was not inherently a ruthless or violent person. He seemed indeed to be a mild man who liked roses and children; in fact he seemed almost absurdly timorous.

He came again to the office the next day and in that conversation I discovered that he knew a great deal about me, among other things that my late husband had started a newspaper, the *Atlanta Voice,* and that I sometimes traveled with Mrs. Martin Luther King, Jr. This frightened me because of the Klan connection and I asked him why he had sought all this information. His answer was merely that he wanted to know something about my background.

The following Monday he was back at my office yet again, and because I had begun to think that somehow we were trying to have a dialogue of importance, I made notes about that visit after he left my office.

"How was your weekend?" he asked me.

"Oh, I had a party at my house," I replied. "It was a bit hectic, preparing for it, but I enjoyed it."

"Did you have many people?" he asked, and I said yes.

"Any white people?"

"Yes, several."

He looked hard at me, incredulously. "You mean you had white people coming to your house and eating at your table?"

"That's exactly the way it was," I said. "And I assure you we found pleasure in being together."

"If the races mix like that," he said, sounding very much the Grand Dragon, "don't you think it will result in an inferior breed of people?"

"The people didn't come to live at my house, Mr. Craig," I countered. "But to answer your question, the answer is no. As far as my study shows, there are no 'pure' races. There are no blood types that correspond to skin color. There is only one race, the human race. There are no proofs that any racial group is inferior or superior to another. And I have never heard of any proof that children born of mixed marriages are inferior or superior biologically. There are white geniuses and morons, and black geniuses and morons, and geniuses and morons who are the children of mixed marriages. You really have no point in that argument."

The Grand Dragon seemed bewildered at this line of reasoning. I noticed his eyes as we talked; they were remarkable, shrewd and luminous, never at rest. His voice was high pitched but not unpleasant. He answered me finally: "But bluebirds and sparrows don't get together in the same nest," he said, "and where in the Bible do you find anything against segregation?"

"There is a great deal in the Bible about concern for our fellow man," I told him, "the importance of the human being, love and charity, the fatherhood of God and the brotherhood of man. How can you make segregation harmonize with these precepts?"

This was one of many conversations. I learned along the way that the Grand Dragon was one of the people who had found segregation profitable; he was out to make the most of his organization. The mere name Ku Klux Klan made me shudder. I associated it with murder and lynchings of blacks throughout the South and elsewhere. I knew that at the peak of Klan activity there had been as many as 150 deaths per year. Yet as one leader of this revived group, Calvin Craig brought to it a peculiar kind of mysticism. He seemed both a super-opportunist and a pragmatist, a man with a sense of crisis, and even with his twisted and misshapen outlook I could still see how he might be regarded as a thoroughly engaging personality.

Sometimes he would say to me that segregation was the only way for the black and white races to live together, and he insisted that it was better for black people that way. He had statistics on how many blacks owned homes in New York and Chicago, and he would declare that there were considerably more blacks who owned their own homes in Atlanta than in many northern cities. Therefore, he argued, blacks fared better under segregation.

"What a cruel way of applying statistics," I told him. "You forget human needs, and you know full well that there is segregation in both the North and the South. In the North it is more subtle, but the lack of well-paying jobs for blacks and the high cost of even poor housing are very real problems. All of this has been a factor in keeping black people endlessly in the ghetto. In the South we had to go to banks operated by blacks and they had to give us preferential treatment in order to make a mortgage loan possible.

"Yet the black man faces a more difficult time in the North because he is not able to define his barriers. In the South many people still remember the signs over the doors and on water fountains, over elevators, inside streetcars and buses, signs reading 'colored' and 'white.' In the North the door to opportunity was closed, but blacks were not always aware that it was closed. Blacks everywhere have suffered numerous blows from bullies and haters who all but obliterated their self-esteem. Even trying on shoes, getting a fountain soda, boarding a bus, to say nothing of voting or getting into college or buying a home — all these have been painful experiences for blacks trying to grow as human beings. People must have self-esteem; they must believe in their own worth and in the worth of others."

I remember I concluded, "Mr. Craig, I hate to see you take numbers and apply them to people that way."

On another occasion, he began an attack on the black press, charging that it resembled the Communist Party's *Daily Worker* in its inflammatory bias in the treatment of news. "The communists think segregation is wrong and so do the liberals," he told me. "Aren't the liberals just following the communist line?"

"Long ago," I said to him, "our Lord worked for brotherhood and for the acceptance of all people as children of God. Does this, now, make him the First Communist? It is to me a strange and sad thing to see many people who call themselves 'anti-communist' credit communism with all the good and constructive beliefs and acts which mankind has so laboriously achieved."

This seemed somehow a momentous revelation to the Grand Dragon, as if he had simply never thought of it that way. It was curious. I had learned enough about Craig to know that he was a shrewd man in many ways, having survived numerous purges and factional fights with the Ku Klux Klan. I had also heard people label him a "redneck," a term implying certain primitive qualities of mind and behavior, and I suppose in truth he had absorbed many of the stereotypical attitudes of rural Georgia. But I had begun to hope, even if presumptuously, that Calvin Craig might begin to see black Americans with fresh eyes, and I dared to hope also that our discussion might result in a new use of his interests and energies.

One day he called me to say that he had just gone through an unusual experience. He had been driving along a certain street in Atlanta when he had seen a black man picking food out of a garbage can, and the sight moved him to stop and get out of his car and walk over to the man to ask why was he doing this. The man replied simply that he was hungry. Mr. Craig then took the man to a Howard Johnson's restaurant and paid the check for a full and adequate dinner. Subsequently, he took the man to the Poverty Center and made arrangements for him to have continuing public assistance. "I am beginning to see people as human beings since I've been talking with you," he told me. "I guess I could have noticed people picking food from garbage cans before," he said, "but I had not bothered to notice."

The Public Accommodations Act had recently passed, so that restaurants were legally required to serve all people regardless of race. The Ku Klux Klan, however, sometimes marched in front of certain restaurants in their white robes, which was also legal but was clearly intended to discourage black people from patronizing such establishments. "What annoys me greatly," I told the Grand Dragon, after he told me about taking the hungry black man to Howard Johnson's, "is how you can don those ghostly sheets to intimidate people and prevent them from going into a restaurant to eat."

"The restaurants hire us to do that," he said flatly. "We are just doing what we are paid to do."

I knew Craig was an active member of the Adair Baptist Church, with its beautiful sanctuary and neatly trimmed shrubbery. "What do you talk about in your church?" I asked him one day. "How do you respond when your pastor reads Biblical passages about loving your neighbor as yourself? The Bible does not advocate segregation and indifference towards other people."

"Don't your people like to be separated?" he countered. "You go to a segregated church, don't you?"

"Yes," I said, "many black people do. Like all sensitive people, we prefer not to go where we may be snubbed or insulted. There are other reasons, too, for our tendency to withdraw. We were compelled by law to stay out of certain parks, recreational centers, concert halls, schools attended by white people, barred by custom from most white churches, and we have had few opportunities to make friends across these barriers. Many blacks have no desire to become acquainted with people who put such a high premium on their whiteness. Such feelings are natural, even if a bit unfair to the majority of whites who are not arrogant, who do not overesteem their whiteness, who are usually friendly and decent. You can hardly blame blacks for wanting to worship in their own churches when they have this unpleasant image of white people. There is a real need for help here, and each of us can do something to better the relationship. I don't see you any more as the Grand Dragon; I see you as a man who needs the love of God, and God can help you over these barriers if you are only willing to let Him."

I began to notice what I thought was a change in Calvin Craig at our Model Cities meetings. He would never sit next to blacks at first, but now he began to sit with them, a bit uncomfortably perhaps, and he began to talk to them.

Ralph McGill, legendary editor and publisher of the *Atlanta Constitution*, kept up with a lot of things in the community, and he had some idea of how this dialogue between me and the Grand Dragon was developing. "In the past I named you 'The Communicator,'" he said to me, "now I dub you 'The Dragon Slayer.'" Others told me, "I think you are causing him to come out of those sheets." An anonymous member of the Ku Klux Klan telephoned me to say, "You are doing a wonderful thing with Calvin Craig. Keep it up. You've got a positive attitude, and you're making him appear the nice man he is." Another called and said, "Calvin Craig has told me some beautiful things about you. I wanted to know if you really are black. I've known him for sixteen years and I have never before heard him say anything good about a black person." There was a pause and then the caller added, "All Klan members are not bad."

It was a bit later that Calvin Craig asked me if I could keep a secret. I said yes, but then he could not tell me just yet. I wanted to know why. "I just can't," he said, leaving me puzzled.

The following weekend he announced his secret: he was leaving the Ku Klux Klan. Several things had happened, he said, which brought him to this decision. He mentioned me as one of them, saying at his press conference that his contacts with Xernona Clayton were responsible for his change in thinking.

The *Atlanta Constitution* published the story first. Then I had a call from a *New York Times* reporter saying he had seen the account on the wire services and wanted to check on the facts. It was a true story, I told him. Calvin Craig was also interviewed on television, again announcing that he was leaving the Klan.

The idea that a Grand Dragon of the Ku Klux Klan had deserted the white robes because of the influence of a black woman seemed either to appeal mightily or offend mightily, and something like pandemonium broke loose. Individuals, news organizations, and assorted groups from all over the country picked up on the story. Calvin Craig's address was not listed in the telephone book, so many of his telegrams and letters were mailed to the mayor's office in City Hall. Messages began to stack up there until finally someone suggested that Xernona was apparently in touch with Mr. Craig, so why not send all the mail to her? Telephone calls were also directed to me, and I simply passed on the messages. Mayor Ivan Allen observed, "Only in Atlanta could the contact for someone in the Ku Klux Klan be a black woman."

Needless to say, all of the calls were not friendly. One black man called me to say that he was thoroughly disgusted with me for having a picture taken with Calvin Craig. He further declared, "A white man can get a black woman to do anything."

Mr. Craig seemed pleased that I was willing to handle his many calls, and I booked him for radio and television appearances in New York, Boston, Kansas City, Los Angeles, and some smaller towns. I even accepted or rejected appointments and interview requests without consulting him. That may sound a bit imperious, but he was somewhat shy about these matters and he didn't like talking directly with callers, so he trusted me to make such arrangements. I did the bookings and later told him where he was to go and what he was expected to do. Among other things, I taught him to say *Negro* instead of *nigra*. This was during the heyday of the civil rights crusade and many things were changing, including the vocabulary of the movement. In New York, Craig ran into difficulty with one audience by using the term *Negro* when he was expected to say *black*. When he returned to Atlanta, he said, "Why didn't you tell me?"

Calvin Craig's office was burned in the civil disorders that followed Dr. King's assassination, but he nonetheless went on television urging citizens of Atlanta to remain calm and not lose their reason. "We must not harbor any hatred now," he declared. "This is what violence has done and this is what violence always does." Craig did not attend Dr. King's funeral, but a few days later he drove out to the cemetery to pay his private respects.

Calvin Craig was investigated by the Federal Bureau of Investigation a few months later, and I was surprised when FBI agents came to my office to question me about him, his background and activities, his personality and his current attitudes about black people. They had first done a five-day investigation of *my* background, presumably to assure themselves that I had no subversive connections. I never knew what the exact charges against Craig were, but the FBI indicated that they were serious and could lead to a prison term. As it turned out, my perception of Calvin Craig's change of attitude may have made the difference between his going to jail or not. At least, the FBI men told Craig that my word about him would make the difference in whether they pursued the investigation or not. The final decision was in his favor, and Mr. Craig called to thank me.

• • •

The young men that I had asked Labor Commissioner Caldwell to help find jobs had worked out well, and the commissioner had told me that he was pleased with Model Cities and the experiment.

Five of the young men worked as supervisors, foremen overseeing the other workers in cleaning Atlanta streets. They were working hard and proud of themselves, but soon they became disenchanted with the low pay and asked me if I would try to get them at least a small raise.

Commissioner Caldwell had always offered a most sympathetic ear to anything I had to espouse; he used to tell me that he was *always* braced to say no to me until I really pressed him with the problem to solve, and then he would end up saying yes. So I always approached him with confidence (though I must add that I always tried to approach anything I undertook with confidence). The young men cleaning the streets deserved at least a modest pay boost, I thought, and I called Mr. Caldwell and suggested we have lunch, that I had an important matter to discuss with him.

We couldn't work out having lunch and decided instead to have dinner at the Marriott Hotel, not far from the State Capitol complex. This was one of the earlier new hotels built when Atlanta started its overhaul of downtown. It was a good place to meet; I had gone there regularly and knew the hostess and waitresses. Commissioner Caldwell picked me up and we went to dinner in his car.

I remember the weather that evening. It had begun raining as we went into the restaurant, a nasty night. We had dinner and talked about potential raises for the young men cleaning the streets, and we talked about Model Cities and about how to deal with the hardcore unemployed. That was a topic of considerable national debate at the time, people wondering and worrying about how to cope with hiring the hardcore, and I remember Commissioner Caldwell and I got into a deep discussion about what else we should try to do in Georgia.

The hostess of the restaurant knew me well and also knew my relationship with the Kings because I had eaten there several times with Martin and Coretta. She came to the table and silently handed me a note.

I opened it and saw the words, "Did you hear about Dr. King?"

I folded the note up again nonchalantly, but the hostess hovered nearby and approached the table again. "Did you read the note?" she wanted to know. "We heard that Dr. King had been shot."

To tell the truth, I just shook my head — in total disbelief. I had just taken Dr. King to the airport, and I had talked to him on the telephone that morning. Of course, a person can get shot in an instant and I suppose I was not thinking logically, but in that moment I could not believe that anything so terrible had happened.

There was even one quite logical reason that my mind rejected the idea. I had literally been in Martin's presence three or four times when we received a report that he had been harmed. Once in Los Angeles, I remember vividly, there was a rumor that some man was planning to blow up Dr. King with dynamite when he came to the city for an appearance. Security was exceedingly tight, but I managed to get through to visit with him, and we were together when the radio reported that the man had succeeded, that Dr. King's car had been blown up. Rev. Abernathy was there, along with others, and we all laughed uproariously because there we were looking face-to-face at Dr. King at that very moment.

There had been other times, too, just like that, so I could reasonably dismiss the note in the Marriott restaurant. I told the hostess and Commissioner Caldwell about the many rumors in the past and that I did not believe this one could be true. But then I thought I really had better check and went to a pay telephone to call Coretta at home.

Coretta had two telephone numbers, both unlisted, and I tried them both and both were busy. This was most unusual. I could almost always get through on one line or the other, so after trying several more times I went back to Commissioner Caldwell and told him about the busy signals. I told him I felt some concern now because both lines were tied up.

It was still raining, and Commissioner Caldwell suggested that he drive me back to my car, thinking we could both listen to the car radio and find out if there were any truth in the rumor. It was a good idea but it did not help. The rains were heavy and there was a lot of weather interference. We tried all up and down the dial; sometimes we got reports of a rumor that Dr. King had been hurt, followed by the disclaimer that the radio newspeople did not yet know if it were true. "That's the rumor," the broadcasters kept saying, "but we do not yet have any confirmation." It worried me more and more, though, that such a rumor appeared to be so widespread.

It worried Commissioner Caldwell too. "I'm not going to take you to your car," he said. "I think you should go by Mrs. King's house. If everything is all right, I'll take you back to pick up your car."

Martin and Coretta lived on Sunset, just west of downtown Atlanta near the Atlanta University complex. We saw Coretta as we approached the house. She had just gotten into a police car with Atlanta Mayor Ivan Allen, Jr. Mayor Allen had received an official report from Memphis authorities that Martin had been shot and had rushed to Coretta's home to take her to the airport to fly to Memphis.

Thirteen

I have reflected often that on that sad night a white elected official, Georgia Labor Commissioner Sam Caldwell, was concerned enough to become practically my personal chauffeur and that another white elected official, Atlanta Mayor Allen, hurried to Coretta's home to offer to drive her to the airport or do anything else he possibly could. It was a time of racial tensions and racial hate, as the shooting in Memphis made abundantly clear, but it was also a time when whites and blacks of good will were trying to build bridges of understanding.

Coretta recognized me in the Caldwell car as she and Mayor Allen were backing out of the driveway. They stopped and she said she had been trying to reach me. Something had happened to Martin, she said, and she had to go to Memphis, but the four King children were at home, and she was worried about them and hoped I would stay with them. She said she would feel better knowing that a close friend was there. She also wanted me to check on Daddy King, she said, to be sure he was all right, because all they knew at that moment was that Dr. King had been injured but the reports were so sketchy that it was unclear how serious it might be. Coretta believed it serious enough, however, that she needed to fly to Memphis at once, so she dashed for the airport with Mayor Allen in the police car and I went into the house to be with the children.

Coretta never got on a plane that night. By the time she reached the airport, it had been confirmed that Dr. King was dead, so she immediately turned around to return to her home and children. She called first from the airport to tell me the terrible news, and she said she was all the more worried about Daddy King. She wanted me to check again that the children were all right, without telling them anything, and then go make sure that Martin's father was all right, too.

Commissioner Caldwell was still volunteering as my chauffeur even though Daddy King lived quite a distance away, and we drove to his home in the rain to see how he was doing so that I could give Coretta a first-hand report.

A lot of people were already gathering at Daddy King's house, the grim word about what had occurred in Memphis having spread rapidly. He was sitting in the kitchen when I got there, seeming calm and composed, but he spoke up sharply when he saw me, calling me by my nickname. "Oh, Big," he said, "I am so worried about the grandchildren; I want somebody there to be with them, somebody they can be comfortable with." I told him that I had just been there and that Coretta was on her way back home from the airport; I said that Coretta especially wanted me to check on him, and then I would go back to stay with the children, too.

"Tell her I'm going to be all right if the grandchildren are going to be all right," he told me. As I sat with Daddy King for a while, he kept saying, "Oh, Lord have mercy," in a low prayerful way. There were no outbursts, no emotional display, only a kind of quiet beseeching — "Lord have mercy." "I'll be all right," he said again as I left, "but I'm worried about the grandchildren." The whole King family was of course stricken with the news of Martin's death, but I thought it was wonderful how everybody was worried to be sure that everybody else was all right. There were strong threads of loving mutual concern woven throughout the fabric of that family.

Daddy King and Mrs. King, Martin's mother, had been at the Ebenezer Church when they first heard word of the shooting in Memphis. A woman in a car driving by had stopped when she saw them outside the church and yelled something at them. They did not quite understand her message, but it had seemed urgent, so they hurried on into the church to turn on the radio and then first heard the report of the shooting. Now, back in their own home again, their friends were gathering to comfort them, and I felt sure that they were going to be all right.

Commissioner Caldwell was still chauffeuring me, so we hurried back in the rain to Coretta's house. As soon as Coretta arrived, she wanted to know how the children were. The youngest child then, Bunny, we called her, though her real name was Bernice, was only five years old and too young to understand much. Her brothers were a little older, Dexter seven and Martin ten, but not able to fully understand either. Only the oldest child, Yolanda, at twelve, was mature enough to really comprehend what had happened. Coretta wanted to talk to the children, but she didn't want to tell them yet exactly what had happened; she was trying to think of the best way to go about it.

There was already so much going on at the King home, people coming and going and a lot of confusion, that Coretta retreated into her bedroom to think about the most pressing thing on her mind. She had gotten more than enough advice as to how and when she should tell the children; some said wait until the next day, some said tell them now, and everybody had a different opinion. Coretta has always been an individual who likes to weigh her own decisions carefully. She makes up her own mind and does what she thinks is best as she sees it, so she went to the privacy of her bedroom to think the problem over, and I sat there with her. Finally she said to me, "I think I am going to tell them now, and I want you to go in with me." But before we had a chance to go anywhere, there occurred a moving scene in the bedroom with the oldest child, Yolanda. I still relive those moments as perhaps the most emotional time during that long night.

Yolanda came into the bedroom to comfort her mother, and the two of them sat there, embracing, on the side of the bed. Yolanda said, "Mommy, I am not going to cry because you are not going to cry. You are such a brave woman, and Daddy told you all the time that this moment might come. I know you are prepared to handle this situation, and, because Daddy always told us that at death we should rejoice, I am not going to cry either."

Yolanda was the first child Mrs. King spoke to directly of the death of their father, though Yolanda was certainly old enough to have already been aware of the news reports. Her comforting speech went on for what seemed a long time. "We are going to get through this, Mommy," she kept saying, "I am going to stand beside you, and you are going to be beside us, and the younger children are going to be okay. They may cry, Mommy," she said, "but you and I are not going to cry." She also kept saying how blessed they were to have had their Daddy for a while, how he had given them so much in such a short time and how that would sustain them. It was a searing and wonderful moment, and they were both crying fully, yet almost as if they were unaware of their own tears.

They embraced again. Coretta was trying so hard to keep herself under control for the sake of the children, and here was her oldest child Yolanda saying how brave they must be and how they would not cry, and the tears were already streaming down both their faces.

"Mama, you have been such a brave wife," Yolanda said, "a good mother, a wonderful companion to Daddy, and we know he is in heaven. Because of your strength you will be able to handle this, and I am going to follow your lead and I am not going to cry either. We will handle this, we will face this together," Yolanda said, and she and her mother both had faces filled with tears.

It is a scene I will never forget, two strong women stricken by the loss of their loved one, each of them attempting to give the other strength and then both of them succumbing to their grief. Such a moment!

Yolanda finished her speech of comfort, and they both wiped the tears from their faces. Coretta was still apprehensive, aware that she needed to talk to the other children but still hedging for a while, hating the idea of having to face that reality. The house was virtual chaos in that period, people everywhere, the telephone constantly ringing, including one call from President Lyndon Johnson in the White House. She had asked the housekeeper to take the younger children to their bedrooms, the two boys Martin and Dexter and the youngest child Bernice. People kept coming into the bedroom and asking, "Well, have you told the children yet?" But she needed just a little more time to dry her eyes and regain her composure.

Finally she said to me, "Well, I cannot put it off any more; I have got to go and tell them," and she asked again that I go with her.

The two young boys slept in the same bedroom in twin beds, and we went to them first. Coretta hesitated as we got to the door, and I could sense a weakening, as if she felt faint. That may have been her most difficult moment since first hearing the devastating news, but she braced herself after the moment's weakness, and I could almost feel the strength returning to her body, the feeling that now she could do it. We entered the bedroom, and she sat down on one of the boys' beds. Coretta asked the housekeeper to leave.

"Your Daddy has been hurt, boys," she started. "He is in Memphis, and he has been hurt." I remember Dexter being puzzled at first and saying, "Mommy, if he has been hurt, why are you here? Why aren't you with Daddy? Why don't you go to him? If he is hurt real bad, Mommy, why don't you go to him?" She hesitated and said, "We'll all go get him and bring him home."

I remember she was stroking Marty's back as she finally told the whole truth: "Your Daddy was hurt badly, so badly that he won't be coming home any more. He was killed," she said. "He died as a result of being shot by a man." Marty and Dexter wanted to know who it was who had hurt their Daddy, and their mother said we were not sure yet. "Was it a bad man?" the children asked. Coretta told them she was not sure if it were someone bad but that there were people who needed help, that their Daddy had tried to help the people who had warped ideas about other people, who had prejudice in their hearts, people who really needed to be healed in their lives and in their hearts, and that was what their Daddy had been doing, trying to heal the sick hearts in our society. "Sometimes that is costly," Coretta said, "and Daddy now has to pay the price for that." But, she said, their Daddy had always known there might come a day like this.

"Then he really is never going to come back any more?" Marty asked, and his mother said, no, not on this earth, but they would all meet their Daddy again in heaven, that when you lived a good life on earth you would have a happy everlasting life with God in Heaven.

Even in that sad overwhelming time, it was interesting to see how the children of differing ages reacted. Yolanda, the oldest, was really almost an adult and understood what had happened and wept together with her mother while they comforted each other. The two boys, Marty and Dexter, understood what was being said to them but did not fully understand its impact. "What will I tell my friends tomorrow at school?" Marty asked his mother, and she told him that he would not go to school the next day. "Oh, Mommy, I have to go to school," he said. "The teacher doesn't want us *ever* to miss school, Mommy; I have got to go." That had to be just about the most difficult moment for Coretta, telling her children that their Daddy was not coming home again and trying to explain that they really did not have to go to school the next day because the family had to tend to certain things, sitting on their bed and rubbing their backs and telling them that their teachers would understand.

She did it all with such dignity and strength, not once giving in to the pain while with the children, though they were firing questions at her rapidly and she was trying to answer each question in a way that they could understand.

"What will we do without Daddy?" one asked, all in concern, as if thinking the whole family would fall apart without their father. "We will manage," their mother told them. "We are going to all stick together. You know Daddy always told us how we need each other, and this is part of what he was always talking about, that we have to share with each other. We love each other and we are concerned about each other, and that means we will survive. We'll make it because Daddy has prepared us, because he knew at some point he might face death. His work has been dangerous, and you know there are a lot of evil things happening in our society. He has faced dangers before, and he was preparing us all along so that if anything ever happened to him we would stick together. And we will. I'll be here for you and we will handle this, and we will get on with our lives the way Daddy would have wanted us to do."

We left the boys then and moved on into Bernice's bedroom, but she was fast asleep and Coretta decided then not to awaken her because she would not have understood much anyway. That proved true the next day, that Bernice at five was too young to understand much at all. She could repeat what was said to her, that her Daddy had been shot, and that Daddy would not be coming back, but she did not really understand.

That night we went back to Coretta's bedroom after she talked to the boys and sat for a while with the door closed. She went to the bathroom for a time too, perhaps as much as anything to be completely alone and regain her composure.

"I *must* notify my mother and father and my brother," she said then, though we already knew that the telephones were a problem. Both lines were constantly ringing, ringing, ringing. Coretta had difficulty in even making an outgoing call because the phone would start ringing again the instant one call was over. Coretta knew that her parents and her sister and brother had almost certainly heard the news from the media, but she wanted them to get the message directly from her. It proved absolutely impossible, though, to get an outside line on her two phones, so she asked me if I would go to my home and use my telephone to contact them. Of course, I said I would.

I was glad to have a chance to go home for a while because by this time my clothes were wet from running in and out of the rain. My trusty chauffeur, Commissioner Caldwell, drove me home, where several people had already gathered. It was a marvelous expression of sharing and caring. These were friends, white and black, who knew my relationship with the Kings and just assumed that I would be busy helping the family, and they came to my house because they wanted to help, too. They knew I lived alone then, since my husband's death, and they came to help by answering the telephone or whatever else they could do.

I did not get a chance to complete the calls to her family because Coretta called me about that time and wanted me to come back to her house and be with her. The two telephones rang constantly, people wanting to express their grief and sympathy, offering assistance in any way possible. There were three calls I remember, those from President Lyndon Johnson, Senator Robert Kennedy, and actor-entertainer Harry Belafonte.

Coretta could not talk to everybody, of course, so we established a system of someone manning the telephones in the kitchen and then connecting the call to Coretta in the bedroom if that seemed necessary. Once, I picked up the phone in the bedroom and was told to tell Mrs. King that the

White House was calling. I took the call, assuming that it would be an aide, but it was that familiar Texas drawl of President Johnson himself, so I passed the phone over quickly to Coretta. He actually mentioned the fact that he had dialed the number himself, rather than having someone place the call for him. He offered comforting words, telling Coretta that he was grief-stricken himself, along with much of the nation and the world. The words were nice, but I thought it significant that he wanted to dial the number himself.

Senator Robert Kennedy was wonderful. We discovered that he had already done things to help, before he had even talked to Coretta, simply because he understood they needed to be done. First, Senator Kennedy said that it was clear that Mrs. King did not have adequate telephone service because his office had been trying to call for several hours and always hit busy signals, so his office had contacted AT&T and made arrangements for someone to come out and add additional telephones. He gave us the name of the man who had been dispatched to attend to that and said the man would be at the King home sometime after midnight. Then, he said, he had heard on the news reports that Coretta was considering going to Memphis to claim Dr. King's body and bring it back to Atlanta, and that being the case, he had already sent a private plane to Atlanta, and he gave us a telephone number and the pilot's name. "The plane is on call and available," the senator said, "and all you need to do is call the pilot and say you're ready to leave." Should the plane not be needed, he added, that was okay, too, but it was there in case.

The third thing that Senator Kennedy had done was probably painful for him because it related directly to the tragedy of his own family. He told Coretta that he knew a great many people, some of great prominence, would want to attend Dr. King's funeral, and he wanted to offer his assistance because he had had to make such arrangements at the time of the death of his brother, President John F. Kennedy. The protocol could be confusing, he said, and he wanted to help. The senator said he had already dispatched three of his staffers to Atlanta and they would set up an office and contact Mrs. King in the morning. "We've had the experience of dealing with a funeral like this," he said, "and we want to share it with you."

Senator Kennedy's call was unique in an important way. So many people called, offering to be of assistance in any possible way. But Senator Kennedy simply understood that certain things needed to be done immediately and proceeded to get them done, even before he could reach Coretta.

The other telephone call I remember from that night was from Harry Belafonte. He was already a huge success as a singer and entertainer and actor, but at the time relatively few people realized how supportive he had been of Dr. King and the civil rights movement. He had performed invaluable services for the Kings over a long period of time. Not only had he marched, but he had raised funds, influenced others to contribute, and assisted in mapping strategies as a member of the SCLC board. He was thinking along the same lines as Senator Kennedy, that Coretta would want to go to Memphis, and he had also arranged for a private plane to be available for her. Beyond that, he and his wife Julie would be in Atlanta the next day, he said, and they would be personally on hand to run errands or do anything necessary to help take care of the arrangements. He didn't ask what else was needed, just told Coretta that he and Julie were on their way, which was wonderfully reassuring.

It was not a night for sleep.

Coretta asked me to plan to meet with the Kennedy staff in the morning as liaison, a conduit through which she could convey her wishes about the funeral and then have them help work it out. One thing I did that night was begin contacting the major hotels in Atlanta, trying to nail down all available rooms for dignitaries who might plan to attend the funeral, and I made plans to meet with the managers of the hotels early the next morning for confirmation.

Sure enough, the telephone representative whom Senator Kennedy had promised showed up around 2:30 a.m. and in a matter of minutes put in six telephones—instead of the existing two—which ended our communications bottleneck.

That first twenty-four hours after the tragedy required a great many decisions, and our first thoughts were of trying to put things in motion, deciding the priorities. Coretta and I were up all night, trying to project what she needed to do. She was in constant contact with advisers like Andrew Young, Dora McDonald (Dr. King's personal secretary), and other SCLC staffers, along with close friends. She was getting advice from all directions on whether she should go to Memphis, whether she should take the children if she did, and whether indeed it was safe to go to Memphis, the city where her husband had been murdered. There were a lot of decisions that only she could make throughout that hectic night. She decided finally that she would go to Memphis to bring her husband's body back to Atlanta but would not take the children with her.

One of the things we knew we would have to do was plan her wardrobe for the next few days, given the fact that practically the whole world would be looking at her. As her friend I wanted to be sure we had the proper attire in readiness, so that whatever her schedule demanded, we could handle it. I called a local clothing store manager and explained that I wanted to come and select clothes for Mrs. King and asked if I could work out a payment plan later. I wanted to be very sure that her wardrobe needs would be met and that she would not have to worry about that herself, nor about the immediate cost. We were also talking about the larger issue of just what kind of funeral it should be, decisions that had to be made as soon as possible so that we *could* plan.

So much would have to be crammed into the next few hours. Coretta knew that the Ebenezer Church would probably not be large enough to accommodate all the people who would want to attend Dr. King's funeral, and yet it was the church where her husband, his father, and his grandfather had all pastored. That was one of her first decisions, a deeply felt one, that she wanted the funeral to be in that church, whatever its limitations. But there might be other ways for a great many people to participate, as many as wished, a way that would also echo her husband's work and commitment, perhaps a march from the church to Morehouse College, another place which had great meaning in Dr. King's life.

She became more and more certain that she wanted such a march, and she looked at me, remembering how Martin had so often teased me, and said, "This time maybe you'll march." I nodded and said yes, knowing that this time I wanted and needed to march, from Ebenezer Church through downtown Atlanta and over the hill to Martin's beloved Morehouse College.

Fourteen

Mrs. King had decided to fly to Memphis to bring her husband's body back to Atlanta, but other decisions loomed. There were black morticians all over the country who offered to help. It was known by this time that Dr. King had been shot in the face and that it would take the craft of a skilled mortician to restore the face for viewing.

A leading mortician in Detroit contacted another well-known mortician in Los Angeles, a friend of mine named Leon Harrison. Leon caught up with me on the telephone and said that he and other morticians over the country had conferred by phone and wanted to come to Atlanta and volunteer their skills to make sure Dr. King looked all right for the funeral. They wanted so much to participate, to express their love for Dr. King, and I thought that was wonderful.

I passed all this information on to Coretta. The Kings have always been a very loyal family to their friends, however, and there was a mortician in Atlanta who was a family friend and a member of Ebenezer Church, so the King family thought it appropriate to put him fully in charge of the funeral preparations.

I tried to help Mrs. King as much as I could with her personal needs, things I could handle so that she would not have to worry about them. As I mentioned, I took over the responsibility of planning her wardrobe for the next demanding days, but Coretta told me she was not sure she could afford the clothes I was telling her she needed. I told her if she would just agree to let me go ahead and get what I thought she required, then I would worry about the cost, and she finally said she would simply leave it all to me.

She did want a veil for the funeral. She remembered the one Mrs. Kennedy had worn at President Kennedy's funeral because it had impressed her with its look of dignity and grace. She didn't want to duplicate that veil; she didn't want anyone to think that she was trying to imitate a Jackie Kennedy look. She simply wanted something similarly dignified and appropriate, yet not a full veil either.

Coretta picked something from her existing wardrobe to wear to Memphis, and I told her that while she was gone I would be preparing some things for her to wear in the next few days and that I would get someone to design a veil like the one she wanted. I was not quite sure where to seek help with the veil, but I thought of a downtown store, Davison's, later bought by Macy's. Yet Davison's had been one of the last holdouts among Atlanta department stores, one of the last to allow blacks to eat in their restaurants and to open charge accounts. Knowing that, I was reluctant to go to them, but then I thought that this was not a time to relive old controversies, and I might find someone at the store who could help me. So I called down there and asked for the millinery department and got a woman—Mrs. Ford was her name—who proved to be wonderfully helpful, the best person I could have found to help with this special request.

I had gotten no sleep through the night and the next morning, and there were so many things to do that it was late afternoon by the time I talked to Mrs. Ford at Davison's. I told her I was trying to design a headdress and veil for Mrs. King for the funeral, that I didn't know exactly what I wanted, but I thought if I could come down and explain it to her that between the two of us we could come up with something that would be satisfactory to Mrs. King. I had already picked a hat from Coretta's wardrobe, a hat I knew was her favorite when we were traveling together, and I thought we could use that as the base for a headdress and veil.

Mrs. Ford was completely sympathetic. It was ten minutes to five that afternoon when I contacted her, and the store normally closed at five, but she said that if I would come around to the back door she would have someone there to let me in and she would try to help. There I was again, I thought, going in through the back door, but at least this time in a good cause. Actually, there was something moving and thrilling about the woman's interest and concern. I remember thinking how I had only moments before hesitated to call Davison's because the store had been reluctant for so long to treat black people equally, and yet now the same store was making a special arrangement to let me in after closing time to help prepare for Dr. King's funeral. My good friend Lillian Lewis accompanied me.

Mrs. Ford and I sat down, and I described the kind of veil Mrs. King wanted. "I think I understand," she said, and she promised she would take an appropriate fabric home with her that evening and put a design together for me to consider. She knew there wasn't much time, that it had to be done in haste, and she called me the next day with a tentative headdress and veil. It proved to be exactly what Mrs. King wanted.

Volunteers in great numbers turned up on the first day after Dr. King's death, offering to do anything that might be needed. It was impossible even to know all of them by name in those hectic few days before the funeral. The Atlanta police had set up tight security so that no one could enter the King home without careful checking and identification, but even so there was not time really to recognize and acknowledge all the volunteers—even some of the most prominent ones.

We had arranged the Kings' dining room as a work station. Letters and telegrams were coming in from all over the world, and the six telephones were in almost constant use. People wanted information about coming to Atlanta and about the funeral arrangements and about everything else you can imagine. It was perhaps the second day after Dr. King's death that I walked outside for a moment and saw someone I recognized, G. Mennen Williams, a powerful figure in the national Democratic Party at that time, a man who had been governor of Michigan for ten years and was then in the U.S. State Department. He was standing under a tree, just standing there, with no one noticing him but apparently not waiting to be noticed either.

I went over and introduced myself and told him I was representing Mrs. King. I explained that it was not possible for her to see everybody but I knew she would want to speak to Governor Williams. He shook his head. "I've already signed the book," he told me, "and I don't want to disturb her. She'll see later that I was here."

In addition to our work station in Coretta's home, Senator Robert Kennedy's staff had set up its operation in the basement of the West Hunter Street Baptist Church, Rev. Abernathy's church. I worked with them on protocol regarding the people who wanted to attend, and we got the managers of all the major hotels to agree to let no rooms without getting my approval. We had to be certain that we could provide space for those who really should have been there. Dr. King wanted all people to be treated equally, but this was one time when some kind of protocol was necessary.

Many other decisions had to be made, even while the preparations for the funeral were going on. The march planned in Memphis, of course, had been interrupted by Dr. King's death, and now the people involved in the preparations for that march kept calling, saying they desperately needed to know if they should continue, or postpone, or even call the march off. Many advised Mrs. King to call it off, but she finally decided, on Harry Belafonte's recommendation, that the Memphis march needed to go forward. She felt that Dr. King's work would be incomplete if that march did not take place. So she said, "Let's keep the march as scheduled, and I will go march in Martin's place."

I was still trying to plan Coretta's wardrobe, thinking this was one task I could shoulder so that she would have one less thing to worry about. I had already told her not to worry about cost either, which I knew she was inclined to do, so I went to two friends who were there by that time, Harry Belafonte and Stan Levinson, a friend from New York who had been very supportive of Dr. King, and I told them I wanted to buy proper clothes for Mrs. King. They both said to go ahead and spend whatever I thought necessary and they would cover the cost, and they even asked if I wanted the money on the spot. "Whatever you think she needs," they said.

The first place I tried was a good women's store on Peachtree Street called Joseph's, located where the Peachtree Westin hotel is now. I had met Mister Joe, as everybody called him, and I knew he had quality clothing. I remember I picked out two fine dresses there, feeling relieved that I didn't have to worry about the expense. I bought other clothes, too, based on what Coretta's scheduled activities were, all the while grateful for Harry and Stan's assurances: "We want Coretta to look nice, and we don't want her to worry about it; just let us know how much money you need."

I remember going back to Mister Joe's to pick up those two dresses and explaining that I had worked out how to pay for them. But Mister Joe refused to take any money. "This is a time when everybody should do whatever they can," he declared. "I own these clothes; they are mine, and I can do this." He even asked me not to tell anyone because he did not want any recognition. "You get so frustrated at a time like this," he told me, "because you don't know what to do, but I can do this."

Coretta was pleased with the things I selected. I knew her size and what I felt would be appropriate for her, and when I look back at the photographs even now, I reminisce about how I chose this dress or that. It made me proud that people did talk about how good she looked in those difficult days. I would buy things sometimes for the next day and wait to find a propitious moment, usually late at night when everything had settled down, to show them to Coretta. She had given me a charge card to use, and I was happy to be able to tell her that I had not used it *once*, that she had good friends who refused to let her worry about these things, and at the same time I did not even tell her who was paying the costs.

Despite our struggles with protocol and hotel rooms for dignitaries, the available rooms ran out quickly. So some of the downtown churches volunteered to make a place for people who wanted to come but didn't have a place to stay. They rented cots and made pallets and served food in the churches for those many, sometimes quite ordinary people who were determined to come to the funeral but had nowhere else to stay that week.

The program for the funeral was a chore for Coretta, long and arduous, because she was trying to meet so many varying needs in arranging who would speak, who would sing, how people could participate. The demands were endless because Dr. King's life had touched so many. He was a minister, so of course the clergy wanted to take part. He was a Baptist, so the Baptist Convention wanted to participate. He was an Alpha, so that fraternity wanted a role. He was a Morehouse man, so that college wanted to be involved. He was a peacemaker, so there were those in the Vietnam peace movement who wanted to be there. He was the champion for civil rights and human rights and better race relations and for unions and for little people and big people. It was as if he represented everybody, and everybody wanted Coretta to let them be part of the funeral program. Yet she wanted to keep it simple, ever mindful of Dr. King's expressed wish to have a simple funeral.

Simply trying to narrow all these demands down to something manageable was perhaps Coretta's biggest problem. It was an absolute impossibility to let all those participate who wanted to do so, and the program ended up being probably too long, even after being narrowed down. Of course there were several phases, the funeral service itself, a service at Morehouse, the burial, so there were ways to spread people out. Also, the body rested in Sisters Chapel at Spelman College from Saturday afternoon until Monday afternoon, then was moved to Ebenezer Church for the Tuesday funeral. Tens of thousands of people stood in line to pay their final tribute to Dr. King.

The funeral home was to deliver the body to the chapel at Spelman on Saturday morning, and we learned that well before the body arrived lines of people were stretched out waiting to view their fallen voice of hope. I was with the King family at a meeting at Ebenezer, another family meeting to iron out more of the details for the funeral, sitting there in Daddy King's office, when someone called from the Spelman campus to tell us how many people were lined up, waiting.

The plan had been for Coretta and the King family to go to the chapel and view Dr. King's body first, before others were permitted to pass by. It was early afternoon by now, the delay caused by the many difficult decisions that still had to be made as soon as possible. Coretta felt sympathy for the throng of people standing in line waiting, and was inclined to let the casket be opened immediately so that they could begin to pay their last respects.

But I said to Coretta, "Oh no, the casket should not be opened until you have seen him; the family should see him first. The people waiting in line will wait as long as it takes," I told her, and Coretta finally agreed. It was a fortunate decision, though I did not initially realize how fortunate.

Coretta is such an empathetic person that she always takes other people's feelings to heart, and she was still fretting over the people standing in line at Spelman. So we completed our meeting at Ebenezer as quickly as possible and hurried over to the Spelman chapel. When we got there, we were permitted to enter through a rear door for the private family viewing. There was one photographer, the one asked to be the official photographer for the funeral, and no one else except the immediate King family and a few friends.

It was a shock when we first saw him.

He did not look like the Dr. King I had anticipated seeing. We knew he had been shot but we believed that the damage would have been repaired, his face restored to its normal appearance. His face appeared distorted, though; his jaw looked too big, out of proportion. It made the contour of his face seem somehow wrong.

Frankly, he did not look good, and Coretta and the family were *so* pained—to put it mildly. It was difficult to see him like this, to see that he had been wounded, had suffered bodily harm. I think every family is more eased in giving up a loved one if the death appears painless. People don't want their loved ones hurt or injured, even when taken in death, and the King family was distressed at seeing their loved one that way in the casket. It was reported that Dr. King died instantly, but you can never be absolutely certain of that, and lying there in the chapel he looked as if he had been hurt, that he had perhaps suffered.

My own husband died a little more than a year before, and that was the first time I had ever really dealt with a mortician as a craftsman. Ed was a fair-skinned person, and when I first went to view his body, his face appeared ashen, not at all true to his color in life, and I was so disappointed. I explained my feelings to the mortician and asked if there were not something he could do, and he said yes, of course, that he would take me home and then try to meet my needs and let me come back later. When I returned a few hours later, my husband's face was fine, restored to its natural color. So that experience was in the back of my head; I had learned that something can be done to make the face appear more natural.

In fact, it was the color of the lower part of Dr. King's face that made the problem so glaring. It was not just that the jaw appeared too large, but it had a harsh reddish tint, different from the rest of his face. I remember thinking of the red clays of Georgia that Martin sometimes talked about.

The mortician was on hand to help, and I could almost feel Coretta's disappointment as she looked at Dr. King's face, so I said quietly to the mortician, "Is there anything you can do with the jaw?" I had spoken quietly, so that the members of the King family would not hear, but he answered loudly, arrogantly, "Miss, the man's jaw was blown off and we had to take clay and make a jaw." I thought that was insensitive and crass and crude, and I could tell that Coretta thought it was an awful remark.

I said to the mortician a second time, "Isn't there anything you can do?" He replied bluntly, "The longer the casket stays open, the worse it's going to get." It was clear that he was not going to be helpful or cooperative, and I could only think of those kind morticians over the country who had called immediately after Dr. King's death to offer their services and wish that some of them were nearby.

But I knew I had to do something. I had no cosmetics of any kind with me, so I asked Julie Belafonte and Mama King if either had any face powder, and sure enough they both did. I thought if we could perhaps tone down the redness of the jaw it would be less glaring. Julie is fair-skinned and had a white-tone powder, while Mama King was dark-skinned and had a darker powder. "Let me have them," I asked, and I took a tissue and began to mix them, trying to blend a color that matched Dr. King's face. I did not actually ask Coretta's permission, but I kept one eye on her, not wanting to be overbearing or to do anything that she didn't want. I could tell by her reaction as I was mixing the powders that this met with her approval.

I took a powder puff and began patting the mixture on Dr. King's face, and the more I applied, the better he looked. "Oh, that looks so much better," I remember Harry Belafonte saying. He took out the handkerchief from his lapel pocket and put it under Dr. King's neck and said, "Why don't you let the excess fall here?" So I powdered and brushed, and the extra powder fell into his handkerchief. When we finished, he said, "This is part of history," and he folded up the handkerchief and put it back in his pocket.

The powder covered that reddish tint on the jaw, and it did make Dr. King appear much more natural. I made some more of the mixture a little later and brushed it on again after the body was transferred to Ebenezer Church. It really did make a difference, a significant difference.

The lines of people at Spelman never seemed to end and it was the same at Ebenezer. So many people waited throughout that long night that Auburn Avenue looked as crowded as if it were high noon. In fact, the lines at Ebenezer were so long that I had to have access to the back door of the church, and I remember that my close friend Lillian Lewis (wife of now-Congressman John Lewis) and I took some prominent persons in that way, including Sidney Poitier and John Johnson of *Ebony* magazine. Many of us went down to the Marriott restaurant after viewing the body, the same restaurant where I was sitting with Labor Commissioner Sam Caldwell when the first word of the Memphis tragedy reached me. It was crowded through the night, people meeting and greeting. We were just too charged up to eat or sleep. I stayed up until almost daylight and then went to Coretta's home and took a quick shower. A woman who worked for me then brought over the clothes I would wear to the funeral. I had been so busy in that first forty-eight hours that I had never even been home to change. I had worn the same clothes for two days.

There were so many people coming and going, so many of the nation's leading figures who wanted to see Mrs. King to pay their personal last respects. I remember when Mrs. Jacqueline Kennedy came by Coretta's home and they embraced at the door of her bedroom. I don't recall the words, but it was the one encounter during that time when the embrace of two women who had suffered a comparable experience seemed to wipe out the need for any words.

Former Vice President Richard Nixon also wanted to speak to Coretta. Nixon's political comeback was well under way by that April of 1968. He had been defeated for the White House by President Kennedy in 1960 and then lost his race for governor of California in 1962, but he had worked steadily in Republican party circles, speaking all over the country, often campaigning for other GOP candidates, taking positions on issues, and by the spring of that year he was considered well on his way to winning his party's nomination for president. So even though Nixon had not been a supporter of Dr. King, his request to see Coretta was weighed objectively.

Ralph McGill, my close friend at the *Atlanta Constitution*, called me about it. McGill had met Mr. Nixon when he was vice president, and Nixon called McGill to ask the publisher if he could arrange a visit with Mrs. King. No, McGill told him, he was not sure he could arrange it, but he had a good friend who at least could find out if it were possible. McGill had trouble locating me; he called several different places and left messages that it was urgent, that he needed to reach me. Would Mrs. King see former Vice President Nixon? he wanted to know. Also, his wife Pat wanted to come with him.

Right away some people at Coretta's home advised her against seeing Mr. Nixon. I did not agree with that and neither did Andy Young. Andy was the one who finally said that this was not the time to be political, and he encouraged Coretta to allow Nixon to come. But he also suggested that she set certain *parameters* for the visit, like saying that he could not bring the press with him or any entourage, that he could not make it a media event in any way.

So my job was to call Mr. McGill back and tell him the visit would be all right as long as it was without press, that it had to be a purely personal visit, without any political implications, and that under those conditions Mr. Nixon would be welcome and Coretta would see him. Mr. Nixon readily agreed and said he considered it a private visit, that he and his wife Pat simply wanted to come.

I must say, honestly, that he went beyond the call of duty in his effort to keep the visit private. Press people hung around Coretta's house constantly, waiting to spot Sammy Davis, Jr., or anyone famous, and they would circulate rumors about when Jackie Kennedy or someone like that was coming by. But on this particular day I told the press that Mrs. King did not expect any other well-known visitors. Mr. Nixon called from the airport and said he was on his way, that he was driving and should be at Mrs. King's home in about twenty minutes. He arrived shortly in an inconspicuous beige automobile, a rental car, I suppose, but not one that would suggest a VIP or anyone official. Mrs. Nixon was not with him, but he was accompanied by an aide who remained outside while he met with Mrs. King.

As planned, I greeted Mr. Nixon outside and escorted him into the house, then left him for a moment in the living room while I went to tell Coretta he had arrived. She asked me to bring him to the bedroom, where they would have privacy. She was sitting on the bed, and he sat in a chair beside her, quite close, talking to her face to face.

He expressed his sadness and sympathy and regretted that Mrs. Nixon had been unable to come with him. One of their daughters who was living in New York had gotten sick the night before, and his wife had felt she needed to go look after her.

Then, the soon-to-be president made a quite remarkable offer. He understood clearly how Dr. King had felt about him politically, Mr. Nixon said, but this was not a political visit; this was a personal visit, and at such difficult personal times people have to do what they feel they should do under the circumstances. "Mrs. Nixon and I did not want to come to offer you any message politically," he said, "but we wanted to offer our personal support in this awful situation. And while people are in a quandary as to what to do at such a time, Pat and I have talked about it, and we want to offer you our personal wish to pay for the education of your children."

Nixon said he knew that Mrs. King must now look after four young children, and he and Pat wanted to help by making funds available to pay for their college education. "If you will accept," he said, "all you need to do is let us know at the proper time, but that is what we are prepared to do, our way of trying to express our sorrow."

Mrs. King was surprised yet noncommittal, and I don't know if she ever even considered taking Mr. Nixon up on the offer. Was it a cynical offer, coming from a controversial political figure who had not been a supporter of Dr. King? I truly don't think so. For one thing, it never became public, as it surely would have if Nixon were seeking some cheap political advantage.

No, I really think it was a sincere and generous offer and that in a way Mr. Nixon represented a lot of white people who did not like Dr. King while he was living but certainly did not want to see such a man murdered brutally, a man trying to do good. Almost everyone conceded that Dr. King was trying to do good, whether you always liked how he went about it or not. I think that having such a man wiped out like that, so cruelly at such a young age, was embarrassing to the whole country; it was so barbaric to have a citizen of these United States cut down while striving for justice. My feeling is that all white people who had any good will at all in them felt some grief and wanted to do something to lessen that grief, so I believe Mr. Nixon's offer was a serious one.

He was very diffident and courteous in making the suggestion. He said he hoped Mrs. King would accept the offer, but he seemed to understand that she might not be able to. I don't recall the exact words, but he said that he and Pat truly hoped that she would accept but that certainly they would not be affronted if she did not.

Another reason I think it was a serious offer was that Mr. Nixon had done his homework. He even knew the ages of the children, from twelve-year-old Yolanda down to five-year-old Bunny. He said to Coretta, "I know you don't have to deal with plans for their college education today or tomorrow, but I wanted you to know that this is our way of saying how sorry we are and that we want to do something.

"All of us believe in education, and I know that Dr. King did," he said, "and I know that you do, too, as does any loving parent." He even made a little speech about how important education is in the modern world and how he knew that Dr. King would want his children to have the best education possible.

Perhaps Dr. King and Mrs. King had already made some provision for the college education of their children, Mr. Nixon even threw in, but he wanted her to know that the offer from him and from Pat was completely genuine and the funds would be there if Mrs. King ever called on him.

Fifteen

Someone once criticized my friend Ralph McGill as a "Jim Crow liberal," meaning presumably that he was not bold enough in opposing racism and segregation. I never thought that was fair. He was editor and then publisher of the *Atlanta Constitution* in the 1950s and 1960s, the leading editor in the South when civil rights confrontations occurred constantly, and his daily column on the front page of the newspaper often thundered out in favor of decency and justice. Maybe he was not as far along in his thinking as Dr. King at first, but he tried to be fair, and he changed and he grew. Many white readers were incensed at what he wrote, and his life was threatened repeatedly. Another comment made about McGill during that time was, I think, more accurate: he had guts when it took guts to have guts.

Atlanta was blessed with remarkable civil rights leadership in the 1960s, not only Dr. King and the SCLC staff with their national headquarters in Atlanta, but also the young leaders of SNCC, the Student Non-Violent Coordinating Committee, among them Julian Bond, John Lewis, James Foreman and Stokely Carmichael. There were also Roman Catholic Archbishop Paul Hallinan, Rabbi Jacob Rothschild, and Atlanta

Mayor Ivan Allen, Jr., who was the only Southern elected official to appear in Washington to testify before a congressional committee in favor of the Public Accommodations Act.

And then there was Ralph McGill.

McGill won the Pulitzer Prize for a column expressing his outrage after bigots bombed the Jewish Temple on Peachtree Street in Atlanta and a school in Tennessee. He later used his column to express support for the public accommodations legislation. When Dr. King won the Nobel Peace Prize in 1964, many in the Atlanta power structure opposed recognizing King in his home city with a testimonial dinner. McGill became one of the four members of the sponsoring committee and helped make the dinner a sellout success, with close to four hundred people without tickets waiting outside the banquet hall, hoping to get in if there were any no-shows. Later, McGill wrote that Dr. King told him how truly disappointed he would have been if his hometown had let him down.

McGill also wrote, a few days after Dr. King's death in April of 1968, that it was no secret that Dr. King had become deeply concerned about the growing segments in the black community in favor of violence and separation from whites. "Before he returned to Memphis," wrote McGill, "he said that if Memphis authorities did not do what was right in what was much more than a strike of Negro garbage workers, he, Dr. King, feared the policy of nonviolence might never again be useful. Negro militants worried him. He could not agree to apartheid in reverse. Nor could he agree that retaliatory violence made sense.

"So he went back to Memphis. And Memphis stalled. And at last the killer, slave to his own hatreds and guilt, destroyed the one prestigious voice that called for nonviolent action.

"The loss is enormous . . . ."

I first met Mr. McGill through Eugene Patterson, then editor of the *Atlanta Constitution*. McGill had become publisher of the newspaper but still wrote his daily column which ran in the left-hand column on the front page. Patterson also wrote a daily column on the editorial page.

I was chairman one year of the Freedom Fund Dinner held by the Atlanta chapter of the National Association for the Advancement of Colored People, and I realized from others that the NAACP had never really involved the newspaper. I have always believed that in order to get something done you go where the power is, and I thought that if we could interest the newspaper, then the people there would keep abreast of our activities and maybe help spread the word, let the community know that our banquet was a credible and important event.

No one with the Atlanta NAACP had ever tried that before, so I suggested we make an appointment to go see Mr. Patterson. I was really more familiar with Mr. McGill because of his reputation, but I thought of him as being in such a lofty position that we would never get to him, that he was unreachable. So we called Mr. Patterson and said we wanted to meet with him and present him the first ticket for the Freedom Fund Dinner and also to let him know something more about the programs of the NAACP.

He had never been asked for such help before, but he was perfectly friendly and set up an appointment, and finally three of us, Dr. Albert Davis, Mrs. Jondelle Johnson, and I, went down to meet with him. He accepted the banquet tickets, and we took a photograph and later ran the picture in the souvenir program for the dinner.

I found out later that he liked the way I set the tone of the meeting. I guess he was probably glad that we weren't coming down to march around the building, the NAACP being considered much more controversial in the 1960s than it was a little later, but we had made it clear that we were there to have a friendly conversation. He knew about the NAACP, but not about its activities in any detail, so we told him about how we tried to raise money and why the money was important. We explained that we were truly trying to fight injustice and to help people who were not able to help themselves, that we were trying to make it a better world where blacks and whites worked together and lived in harmony.

He was very responsive, and as we were leaving, I said to Mr. Patterson that I wanted to talk to him some time about a different project, not connected with the NAACP but involved with the peaceful integration of residential neighborhoods. This project was directed by SWAP, or Southwest Atlantans for Progress. He was responsive to that, too, and immediately asked his secretary to arrange another appointment at a definite time. I was impressed with that since it indicated that his interest was genuine.

A lot of residential neighborhoods were then going through a difficult time of racial transition, not just in Atlanta but all over the country. One typical pattern was that one or more black families might move into what had been an all-white neighborhood, and then white families would begin to move out, in fear that they might be suddenly surrounded by blacks. Unscrupulous realtors even encouraged this white flight, hoping to buy these white-owned houses at a considerable discount and then turn around and sell them to black families at a premium.

I knew this was wrong, that people could live together without fear if they got to know each other. I was working as community relations director for the American Friends Service Committee when we started SWAP in the mid-1960s, our aim being to try to stabilize one particular neighborhood, Cascade Heights, a middle-class southwest community. Black families were moving in, but there was still a substantial number of white families living there, and our effort was to get whites and blacks together in a friendly way and maintain the neighborhood as an integrated one. We started out with just twenty-two members, yet the group swiftly grew to more than five hundred.

Our first meeting with the initial twenty-two, eleven blacks and eleven whites, took place at the home of a white family.

It was almost funny, really, the way the eleven blacks sat on one side of the room and the eleven whites on the other. I was always thinking of ways to break the ice at such encounters, and one thing I did was to serve coffee with only one spoon on the tray for all to use. Nobody objected or dropped dead or said they worried about germs, even though I had come to realize that some white people truly worried about germs from even this kind of slight contact with black people.

Getting whites and blacks together in that period was one of the most exciting things I was ever involved in. We would talk about the differences in our lives and the things that were similar, and more and more people began coming to the meetings. I was convinced that people might differ in size or height or color, but on the inside people are the same. I also believed that outward diversity provides stimulation and growth. So I went back to see Mr. Patterson to tell him about SWAP, and to my delight Mr. McGill joined us.

I told them both I really needed some help with the SWAP program because trying to stabilize a neighborhood, trying to encourage racial integration, was not easy. I had been to see Atlanta Mayor Allen about it and asked for his help, and he had laughed at me. Not in a cruel way, I don't mean that. But he said, "Oh Ms. Clayton, you haven't been in town very long, and what you don't understand is that a lot of people wish integration would work, but black people prefer living on their side of town and white people prefer theirs. Now, I hate to burst your bubble of enthusiasm, he said, but can you really be serious about this? It's not going to work," he insisted.

"Mayor Allen," I told him, "you have not burst my bubble of enthusiasm; what you have done is expand it, because now I am more determined than ever to make it work. I want to come back to you later and prove that my optimism was leading me in the right direction."

I told Mr. McGill and Mr. Patterson about all this and added that as a matter of fact I thought SWAP was doing well, that we were now meeting at least once each month, and that attendance was growing. Those attending were now talking more openly and honestly about their fears, I said, blacks saying mostly that they did not care if whites lived next door, whites explaining why they *did* care if blacks lived next door. We were having some very healthy and open discussions.

I told Mr. McGill I wanted to invite him to speak at one of our meetings. If he came, I said, it would accomplish several things at the same time. First, it would give him immediate evidence of what we were doing, and, second, the very fact that he had come would help the program. When white people get involved in such projects, I said, it makes them feel better to know someone of consequence is really supportive, that they are not out there by themselves. His visit would also make me feel that I had accomplished something, I added, because I believed it important to get people of influence involved in projects that benefitted the community.

He agreed to come to one of our meetings, which made me feel great, so I went on to expand the invitation further. I asked him, "Have you ever been to dinner at a black person's house?" He appeared vague and then said, no, he was not sure he ever had. So I invited him to come to my house for dinner, thinking that I would also invite some of the SWAP leaders and that after our meal we would all go together to the SWAP forum at Southwest Hospital.

McGill indeed came to dinner at my home on the evening of the meeting—I think I even cooked—and I know he enjoyed himself. It was a thrilling night for all the people there. We talked about Mr. McGill's philosophy, and he congratulated the people involved in the SWAP project. One white couple had brought a copy of one of Mr. McGill's books, and they asked him to autograph the book for their granddaughter. He got more joy out of that than anything else, I think. He really loved young people, and he knew they were our salvation. He often said, "Well, we older types are already set in our ways, and if there is any hope for America, it will be through the younger ones."

Normally during that time we were having from sixty to seventy people attending SWAP meetings. McGill wanted to know how big an audience to expect, so I predicted, knowing that the word would be out around the neighborhood that Ralph McGill of the *Atlanta Constitution* was the speaker, that we might have as many as seventy-five or eighty people.

Fully two hundred people showed up at that session, because so many thought it was wonderful that McGill would come. There were people there who already knew him and wanted to see him again, people who wanted to meet him for the first time, and people who had heard him speak but had never seen him in a neighborhood setting like that. It was regarded as a feather in my cap to be able to deliver him to the meeting, though I suppose few really understood how easy it was. I never would have thought it would be so easy because of the accepted notion that important people are not easily approachable. But McGill certainly was; he was just wonderful.

I knew of Ralph McGill before I came to Atlanta because my husband was already in the city when McGill helped sponsor the dinner honoring King for the Nobel Prize. Back then, honestly, I did not always feel that his columns revealed a clear commitment; I was a private critic really. But after we became good friends, I found that I could mention anything to him.

I was reading the newspaper one Sunday, early in 1968, and I found myself gazing at two pages of pictures of brides. Every single one of them was white. I called Mr. McGill on the spot and asked him, "Don't black girls get married in Atlanta?" "Of course they do," he said, puzzled. So I asked him, "Where are the pictures of black brides? You've shut them out of your newspaper." He really got on that case because on Monday, the very next day, the society editor of the newspaper called me and said she was sending me a note on what a bride needed to do, what kind of information should be sent in and what the deadlines were. "Mr. McGill told me to get this to you," she said, and sure enough it was not long before pictures of black brides also began appearing in the newspaper.

Black people generally identified with McGill and considered him a friend, and I felt that I could go to him with any sensitive issue. For instance, I once called his attention to a story on the front page about a man who robbed a bank. "Look," I said, "the police caught him and he is in custody, so why must you identify him as being black?" McGill had told me earlier that the newspaper had dropped racial identifications in crime stories, unless the suspected culprit was still at large and you needed that as part of the description, but here was someone already in custody being identified as black. In fact, that same day's newspaper had an article on another page about another man committing a different crime, but he was still loose and there was no racial identification that he was white.

So I asked Mr. McGill, "Isn't this inconsistent? You say you have dropped racial identification in stories about crime unless the suspect is still at large, but here the man already in custody is identified by race and the man being sought is not. How did you miss this?"

He would agree, laughing, and say to me, "Oh Xernona, Xernona, you know I don't know, but that is why you are so valuable to us; you help keep us on our toes, and I guess we will have to do better."

He would follow up on such matters, I know, because some of the reporters who were my friends would tell me that McGill had pointed these errors and inconsistencies out to them, maybe in a particular article. I remember one reporter complaining, jokingly, that I had the boss looking at them now. And then sometimes Mr. McGill would call me up and quiz me on stories, to see if I had noticed how well some particular thing had been handled.

Back to that earlier criticism, that Ralph McGill was a Jim Crow liberal because he did not do enough. I don't care what a person does; for some people it can never be enough. His image in Atlanta's black community was wonderful overall, like that of a saint coming on the scene. He was perceived as one of the rare ones of our time, a white person who seemed to have understood, a white man of substance and under-standing and sympathy for the cause of racial justice, a man who in spite of being white somehow understood that the treatment of blacks was blatant injustice. In essence, the black community saw him as a friend.

Just to find a white man in this environment who seemed to understand, even if he didn't do *anything*, seemed almost impossible. It seemed sometimes to blacks that nobody in the white community wanted to understand that there was injustice. Even the white ministers, the voices of Christian fellowship, even they did not understand. Literally, in trying to stabilize the southwest neighborhoods through SWAP, we found white ministers the least cooperative group of people. We were trying to say, let's get together, white and black, let's show that the Christian spirit prevails, and let's do unto others as we want to be done unto, and here were these white ministers who did not even want to understand that we were being done unto with clear injustice. What we were really expecting was to have those ministers follow the guidelines of Christian principles.

So Ralph McGill was appreciated as a person who recog-nized that blacks were being treated unjustly and who declared that it was not right. It did not matter whether or not he marched in a demonstration or beat Ku Klux Klanners over the head. What mattered was that he was there, sym-pathetic, trying to understand, doing more in that way than almost anybody else.

Eleven o'clock on Sunday morning was the most segregated hour of the week, as many observed at the height of the civil rights movement, because that was the hour when most whites and blacks went to their separate churches. And it bears repeating that the white ministers in southwest Atlanta offered little help to SWAP. Mr. McGill, after serving as one of the four sponsors for Dr. King's Nobel Prize dinner, wrote later that the protestant ministers "who were approached to join in sponsoring the dinner retreated in haste with many excuses." Yet I should point out that two of the four sponsors were religious leaders, Archbishop Hallinan and Rabbi Rothschild. The fourth sponsor was Dr. Benjamin Mays, president of Morehouse College, Dr. King's former teacher and mentor and longtime friend.

I still puzzle over those ministers who so resisted change. They were guilty of a blindness, I think, seeing only one side of humankind and only the letter of the law that said there should be separation of the races. They did not deal with the moral issue, the higher law which was the word of God, that everybody should be treated equally because in the sight of God we are all the same. It was easier to look at the immediate, and their immediate thing was the old law of the land, that blacks and whites should remain separate, along with the perception that blacks were inferior and illiterate and unequal. But, again, there were some white religious leaders who showed leadership and goodness in representing the higher law. There just were not enough of them, perhaps because it took courage, real courage.

My friend Ralph McGill had that kind of courage.

Sixteen

My friendship with Ralph McGill led to my breaking another barrier; I became the first black person in the South to host a regular television program.

Mr. McGill said he liked my style in pricking the conscience of white Southerners. Offering those two examples from the newspaper, he explained that I did it in a way that was a little embarrassing but at the same time gentle. So he began recommending me for panels and programs, sometimes when he was asked and could not accept the invitation himself. I have always felt that you don't have to be confrontational, even though I know confrontation can sometimes produce good results. But there are different styles for approaching a problem, and mine has always been, let's reason together. Mr. McGill recognized the problem, saw the need to open people's eyes, and he often selected me to do it because he thought I did it in my own special way. It was very flattering to me, of course, that he felt that my way of pricking the white conscience had some impact.

I really loved him because he seemed so concerned about me, and so sensitive to everything. After I started the television program in July of 1968, he would call up sometimes and say, "Oh, I need a good laugh, let's have lunch." He would call on the spur of the moment, and sometimes I would do the same thing, call him at the last minute and say, "Mr. McGill, I've had a bad busy morning and I'm feeling down, but I know I would feel better if we could have lunch." "Let's see if Grace can change something," he would often say, and he would get his secretary Grace Lundy to change his schedule so we could have lunch.

Once I was on the way to have lunch with him and was at the corner of Broad and Marietta streets when I noticed a man pass me and then stop and turn around so that he was behind me again. He was looking at me hard, and I thought perhaps he recognized me from television. Then he passed me again and brushed up against me hard, really hit me. It scared me even if I didn't register any immediate emotion. I wondered if he had hurt me in some way. I was stunned, I guess, and I hurried on to Mr. McGill's office to tell him about it. I pointed out where I had felt the blow, near the pocket of the coat I was wearing, and Mr. McGill asked, "Do you have anything in that pocket? Maybe the man was trying to pick your pocket." I didn't think I had anything in that pocket, but I reached in to check and found a piece of paper with a note on it. "Call me, baby," the note said, and there was a telephone number. "We'll find out about this," Mr. McGill said, and he went right to the telephone and dialed the number. It was the number of a rooming house, so there was nothing to do but laugh about it. We decided the man had probably recognized me and wanted to be fresh.

We loved to try different places for lunch, and I remember going to the Hyatt Regency hotel when it first opened. Another time we were going to the Midnight Sun and were in Peachtree Center when Mr. McGill excused himself for a moment. I thought he had seen someone he knew and was going over to speak. But he had learned that I loved cheese, and he came back in a minute with a gift for me from the new cheese shop in Peachtree Center. "Here's something I want you to try," he said, "a new cheese I discovered, and you might like it too."

You know, I never ate that cheese because Ralph McGill died four days later, so that was the last thing he ever gave me. I just kept it in the refrigerator until all the mold got to be a health hazard. I guess I was trying to hold on to a last memory of a friend.

But back to that opportunity for me to host a television show. A program sponsored by religious broadcasters was taking place at the Hyatt in Atlanta, and a lot of television people attended, not just those doing religious programs. Someone called me and said Mr. McGill had given them my name and had told them I would be the perfect person as speaker on one part of the program. I accepted readily.

But in the conscience-pricking spirit of Mr. McGill, I told that television group that I didn't understand them. First, I told them, I did not understand religious leaders who would alienate and exclude black people, and second, I did not understand white broadcasters who excluded blacks from their profession. Atlanta was a wonderful city, I said, a popular city, almost an ideal city in its racial mixture. There were black educators and civic leaders and outstanding citizens, along with a white citizenry generally responsive to the needs of the community. Atlanta was considered the coming city of the South, I told them, the city of the future, the city that integrated public schools peacefully and was proud to call itself the city too busy to hate. Yet there were things hard to understand, I said. For example, there was not one single black person appearing as a television broadcaster in the entire city.

Dr. King always praised the media highly, I said, noting the importance of their contributions in the civil rights movement. Were it not for television, he would say, people would not really have understood about the hoses and the attacking dogs and the segregated public swimming pools and all the other things that had such an impact on masses of Americans, white and black. Nothing could portray these things so dramatically as television, and Dr. King understood and valued that. What I found so hard to understand, I told this group, was how a white broadcaster working on a lily-white television station could go out and document these inequities, about black people being shut out of so much, denied access to swimming pools and even water fountains. In a word, I pointed out how the white reporter goes back to the lily-white station and turns the film over to a lily-white editor who gives it to a lily-white writer who turns it over to the lily-white anchor, and then the report is put on the air for the station's audience. "I don't see any difference," I told them, "between shutting blacks out in the general community and shutting them out of the television industry; it's racial discrimination either way."

My speech was received pretty well, I thought, and before I had even gotten back to my office some of the television people attending the meeting had already called Mr. McGill. He called me and said he thought the feedback was positive, even though the people who called him said something like, well, she really embarrassed us. But they went on to say that they were embarrassed mainly because I spoke the truth, there was not one black person regularly on the air on television in Atlanta. He said he told all the people who called that there was one sure way to overcome that embarrassment, namely to put some black folks on the air and break that particular color barrier.

McGill called me again a few days later and said, "Have you heard from anybody with a television station?" I said, "No, what about?" It would concern the speech I had delivered to the broadcasters, he said, and maybe involve something else too. I really thought he meant somebody was going to attack me, critically, for embarrassing them. I learned later that he had talked seriously to the managers of, I think, all three of the main television stations in Atlanta, about my speech and about breaking the racial barrier on local TV.

Channel 2, WSB-TV, said they wanted to do it but not just yet. Channel 5, WAGA-TV, however, was more enthusiastic and told McGill they would like to talk to me about it. H.W. "Buddy" Ray was general manager at Channel 5 at that time, and I remember that he and Paul Shields, one of the station's regular newscasters, invited me to meet them at the Diplomat restaurant for lunch.

That lunch changed my life, sending me off in new directions, and it's funny to me looking back that I had no idea at all that it would. I knew they wanted to talk about the speech I gave to the broadcasters, and almost the first thing they said was that it had been embarrassing for them and they did not want to be embarrassed any more like that. "We want you to help us out," they said, and I anticipated this from what Mr. McGill had said to me, but I was thinking in terms of advising them, supplying them with a list of names of black men and women who might audition to become an on-air television person at Channel 5. I was even already thinking of some names but also thinking that I would not have to give them the list that very day, that I needed to take some time to think about it carefully.

I had been nodding and agreeing as we talked, saying of course I would try to help, but finally I put the question to them, what specifically did they want me to do at this stage of their planning? They said they wanted me to come up with the details and format for a "magazine on the air" or a talk show of some kind. I objected, saying that their first step should be to decide on the person they wanted to host the show and then let that person develop the details and format. They looked at me curiously.

They had already made that decision, they said; they wanted me to break the color barrier on Atlanta television, and it was only then that it finally sank in that they wanted me actually to create and host the new show. Of course it was impossible to say no after all my big talk at the broadcasters' meeting, and I accepted the offer at once. I did raise the

question, though, why me? After all, I had no professional
television experience at all. They were very straight with me.
They were committed to breaking the racial on-air barrier in
Atlanta television, and they knew it would be controversial no
matter how they did it. But they also wanted to play it safe to
the extent they could, meaning they wanted someone who
was already widely known in the white and black communities, who would find broad general acceptance. They
thought I was such a person. It was flattering and the beginning of a wonderful challenge.

Actually, I began to plan the format for the show still half-
thinking I might say to them later that I believed they ought
to consider getting someone with real television credentials.
The traditional format of the talk show is pretty common
now but was relatively new in the late 1960s, so I looked at
what the networks were doing, at some local shows, and
began to plan how I would play hostess. I worked for a time
at developing a proposal, and then we had a second meeting,
this time over dinner at my home in southwest Atlanta.

Now that invitation to dinner proved to have an interesting
impact. I did not plan it that way, exactly; it was just that I
was single at the time after my husband's death, and it was
often easier for me to entertain at home than to go out. I
lived in a beautiful neighborhood, a middle-class black neighborhood, and for Buddy Ray and Paul Shields it was an eye-
opening experience. The houses were neat and clean and nice
with handsome, manicured lawns, and my friends from
Channel 5 were really not aware that such black neighborhoods existed, really no different from comparable white
middle-class neighborhoods. They even asked me when they
walked in if my neighborhood were racially mixed. I said no,
it was all black families.

I was a gracious hostess, if I may say so. I had a good
housekeeper who helped when I entertained, and she did
the kinds of things that Mr. Ray and Mr. Shields were

accustomed to seeing, except I could tell they were not accustomed to seeing them in a black person's house.

We talked about the format for the show. I told them that I wanted everything to be done in really first-class fashion. I wanted a living room set with real furniture, nice furniture, and I wanted good direction and great technicians, the best the station had to offer. I wanted the person operating the camera to reveal the true color of guests who happened to be black. I hated to see black folks on television with their eyes and teeth showing white and their skins not quite right because the cameraman did not know how to deal with the varying hues of black skin. This was important later on because I did run into one camera operator who didn't care about proper coloring and made all the guests come out the same shade of black regardless of their true shades. But I already had that commitment from Buddy Ray, the general manager, and I knew that a camera operator or technician who would not follow my directions on this matter would be dismissed.

We got a lot of people involved after that dinner at my house, planning and getting ready to do the show, which first aired on a Sunday evening, July 21, 1968.

During our California days Ed and I used to go to receptions and kickoff parties for all kinds of things, so as the date for the first show neared I suggested we have a premiere party, with guests who would then be aware of the show and could be our best public relations asset. Buddy Ray liked the idea, so I asked him if he were willing to pay for it. He said, yes, certainly, and I laughed because I told him I thought I knew how to get everything for free. The Paschal Brothers Hotel, a black-owned business, had a wonderful restaurant, and I got them to donate the food, fried chicken and fruit and a lot of other good things, and I had a friend at Delta Airlines who got Delta to donate champagne.

One ugly aspect did arise, illustrating the kind of racial fear that existed then, that still exists sometimes. Some people at the station got nervous and concerned that so many black people would be coming to the station for that first taping since the station was located in a white neighborhood. They were actually afraid that someone might get mad about so many blacks in their neighborhood and come bomb the station, so afraid, in fact, that they begged the management to cancel the party. Management asked me about it, about perhaps putting the show on the air first and delaying the party until later, kind of waiting to see what the reaction to the show might be. I said that I had never heard of a premiere party after the fact of the premiere, but I was sweet about it. The invitations had already gone out, but I said if management wished to call the party off I had friends who would volunteer to send out notes saying the party was cancelled. The station management thought better of that and decided to go on with the party as planned.

So we had Delta champagne to start our television flight and delicious food from the Paschal brothers, James and Robert. Daddy King and Mama King and A. D. King were there, all dead and gone now. So was my Ku Klux Klan Grand Dragon friend, Calvin Craig, and Georgia Governor Lester Maddox. It was interesting that the governor would come because he first became known as an outspoken segregationist, barring blacks from his Pickrick Restaurant. Mr. McGill, bless his soul, had gone off somewhere in Europe and was trying to get back to Atlanta but got detained in New York. He did not make it back in time, and we were both sick about it. However, his wife Mary Lynn, my good friend, was there.

We had people there from the public housing projects, too, as well as people of prominence. There were flowers and telegrams from my friends around the country, like Sarah Vaughn, Duke Ellington, and Lionel Hampton, and I remember that Sammy Davis, Jr., sent a beautiful bouquet.

That first taping was a great success, and it changed the whole complexion, pardon the pun, of my presence on the show. We kicked the show off with an aura of prestige and first-class style and that attitude prevailed until the last day of the show. The fact that I had friends all over the country sending messages to wish me well impressed even the people at the station. Sometimes you can tell someone that you know this person or that person, and the someone assumes that, well, yes, she probably met that person somewhere once but doesn't really know him or her. But we ended up having people like Mahalia Jackson, Harry Belafonte, Sidney Poitier, Carol Channing, Bill Cosby, Lucille Ball, Jesse Owens, Sugar Ray Robinson, Lena Horne, Mickey Rooney, and Leslie Uggams as guests on the show even though it was difficult for a local television show to get such people.

I had written a regular column for the *Atlanta Voice*, called "Themes and Variations," and that seemed a good title for the new half-hour television show as well. The show was scheduled for prime time on Sundays, every other Sunday evening at 6:30 p.m. Guests on that very first show included two youngsters from a new job program, Rent-A-Kid; Dr. Benjamin Mays, president of Morehouse College; and Cecil Alexander, a white liberal Atlanta architect who had taken a progressive interest in housing problems. Actually I had wanted also to have the former Grand Dragon, Calvin Craig, as a guest on that first program, but Mr. Craig was running for a local political office and his appearance would have created a fairness-doctrine problem for WAGA-TV.

The television critics with the Atlanta newspapers were friendly to the new show. Paul Jones, the critic for the *Atlanta Constitution*, wrote a column the week before the show began, noting that I would be the first black person to host a regularly scheduled prime-time television show in Atlanta and listing some of the "big names," as he put it, who had already tentatively agreed to appear on early shows: entertainers Eartha Kitt, Duke Ellington, Mahalia Jackson, Barbara McNair, and Lionel Hampton, plus Whitney Young, then head of the National Urban League, and former heavy-weight boxing champion Joe Louis.

Dick Gray, whose television column "Gray Matter" ran in the *Atlanta Journal*, wrote a glowing review that ran the day after the first show aired. His first paragraph made friendly reference to the women then best known on Atlanta television: "Move over, Miss Anne. Step aside, Eleanor Knight. Don't distract me with your miniskirt, Linda Faye. I have a new lady idol in the local-television department. Her name is Xernona Clayton and she is something else." Gray noted that Channel 5 billed the show as a "special on Negro contemporary life" but it was more than that, he added, since it "gave us a half-hour look at a woman who might turn out to be the first lady of Atlanta television — given enough exposure and enough freedom to do what she wants to do." He went on to say that he had made a list of adjectives to describe my debut as television hostess — sparkling, pixieish, relaxed, friendly, poised, tasteful, gracious, aware, and hip.

That was all enormously flattering and encouraging, but Gray also zeroed in on exactly the worry I had expressed in the early planning, that the technical production of the show be of the highest quality. He noted that neither color nor sound were as good as they should have been, that some kind of background hum interfered with the sound and that the color was not consistent when we shifted from camera to camera. Yet, he concluded, WAGA-TV could surely correct these technical flaws and predicted that the show was "a sure bet for a continuing series."

Some of those early shows were great fun. We had Hank Aaron, the all-time great home-run hitter, on the third show, along with "Malt Liquor" Patrick, one of my street-wise friends, and Georgia Labor Commissioner Sam Caldwell, who worked out the program to hire the young men from those street groups. In October 1968, after the show had been airing for three months, WAGA-TV executives, general manager Buddy Ray and station manager Terry McGuirk, asked me to sign a two-year exclusive contract to continue doing the show.

The show had a one-year birthday party after our first twelve months, and Mr. Ray, who had so encouraged me, appeared on that anniversary program and declared the show now had a new name. No longer "Themes and Variations," now it was simply "The Xernona Clayton Show." In a subsequent column Dick Gray quoted Ray as saying that he had first envisioned the show as a means of communication with the black community, a way of getting feedback from that community.

"Interestingly," Ray went on, "we have gotten quite a bit of favorable feedback from the white community, which means that the program also created an avenue of communication between the two communities." That's what I remember, too, that many of those who called or wrote letters were white people saying that the program had been an educational experience for them. Not all the communications were friendly. One white woman regularly sent in news clippings reporting crimes committed by black people and wrote that she felt sure I would want to call them to the attention of the audience. But I felt it was real progress in overcoming prejudice when any one white person could perceive me as an individual first, not as a Negro first. One white man wrote in that he had become a regular viewer despite racial prejudice. "You teach a lesson without preaching a sermon," he wrote.

Six months after our first-birthday show, we expanded the format to a one-hour program and went into syndication once each month, with the other Sunday show each month remaining a thirty-minute program. A great many people at the station worked hard to make our production of consistently high quality, especially Bob Brennan, who was both station news director and executive producer of our show. WAGA-TV was a Storer station, and other stations in the group put the programs on their schedules, including stations in Detroit, Boston, Milwaukee, Toledo, Cincinnati, and Cleveland.

We had some funny moments doing the show. Once in 1972 the entire cast of "Gunsmoke," one of the most popular TV shows ever and then in its eighteenth year, came to Atlanta and taped a special show that ran as part of our program. Another time, during an interview with Mahalia Jackson, I asked her if she had any advice for young people. Yes she did, she said. She wanted all the young ladies to take care not to eat so much that they would grow up to be fat and have to wear a girdle. "Mine is killing me right now!" she said.

Then there were the children. I loved getting little notes from the youngsters. Here are some samples:

—I like your hair but how do you get it to stay on top of your head? Love, Judy.

—Could you come and have dinner with us some time? When you answer, mark it "Personal" cause I like to get personal letters. Harry.

—We went to see Santa the other day but I didn't feel like talking to him, but I'll write him and tell him to send my presents, anyway.

—I wanted a dog for Christmas but Mommie said we're getting a baby instead. I don't know how that came about.

—How old are you? If you don't want to say, just answer if you are older than Mama . . . she's either forty-nine or thirty-eight, I'm not sure. Love, David.

Reg Murphy, who succeeded Eugene Patterson as editor of the *Atlanta Constitution*, wrote a column in November of 1970, quoting an *Ebony* magazine editorial to the effect that Atlantans suffered no real shock in viewing the South's first black hostess of a TV talk show, since Atlanta had earned its progressive image with a long history of black firsts, but "shocking it was to rural Georgians who are traditionally hostile to most things black. . . ." There was some truth in that, but there was another side, too, a happy side.

One night I did an entire show on ethnic foods, soul food like collard greens, chitterlings, ham hocks, and all the trimmings. Several weeks later, a white couple in rural south Georgia wrote me a letter to tell me that they enjoyed that show so much it prompted them to want to prepare a similar feast for me. The man wrote that this was the first time he had ever invited a black person for dinner and the event would mean a great deal to him and to his wife, so would I please say yes to the invitation. Well, I told my director that the letter was so moving I could hardly say no, in spite of the fact that I don't quite trust white folks to cook collard greens in proper fashion.

The man's letter implored me not to let him down, because watching my show had destroyed his prejudices against black people, but he was getting older and might not live long enough to expiate his past sins. So my producer and I accepted the invitation and went to the man's home for a fine dinner. The man actually wept tears as he explained that he had never had a black person as a guest in his home before. It was a sustaining experience for me, and I knew I was doing something right with the television show.

The show was on the air from 1968 to 1975 and I gave up being a talk-show host only because I wanted to spend more time with my new husband, Judge Paul L. Brady, whom I married in 1974. More about him later.

I was sorry my friend Ralph McGill was not able to get back from that overseas trip in time to attend the taping of my first show, but I am grateful that he lived until February of the next year, in vigorous good health until a heart attack abruptly took him away, and that he lived long enough to see my show become a success. The next February, one year after his death, I ended the show with a tribute to my old friend. I am still grateful to him for his loving encouragement.

Seventeen

Segregation had many hateful aspects, but surely none was much worse than the fact that a poor black woman was permitted to give birth only on certain days, at least if she wanted to have her baby in a healthy hospital environment. That was true until the late 1960s in Atlanta at Grady Hospital, where most poor mothers gave birth.

I had become friendly with a number of black physicians after I moved to Atlanta, as well as with Dr. Roy Bell, a dentist who had befriended my husband Ed when he was first in Atlanta by himself and I had not yet moved from Los Angeles. Dr. Bell and his wife and Ed and I all became good friends, and it was Dr. Bell who came to me, outraged at discovering that there were only certain days of the week at Grady Hospital when black women were admitted to give birth to their babies. It angered me too, especially since the hospital was financed by public funds, and we decided to do something about it.

Now, the fact was that Grady probably would admit a pregnant black woman clearly about to give birth at any minute. But that same pregnant black woman could only be examined for anything related to her pregnancy on certain days, even if she felt a severe labor pain. How can any woman be sure if such a pain means her baby is really on the way? Yet a black woman was not free to hurry to the hospital to be certain.

Dr. Bell was very active in our community, and he is remembered by many as the man who ran his car through the barricade that Atlanta Mayor Allen had set up at Peyton Road. In fact, that story is worth retelling, now that I've brought it up. Setting up that barricade was one of those actions, regardless of the intentions behind them, which instantly produce unforeseen controversies and consequences. Atlanta Mayor Allen was considered a progressive in the black community and had been elected with strong black voter support. He was sympathetic to me when I went to see him about SWAP and told him of our effort to integrate neighborhoods peacefully, even though he was not optimistic about our chance of success. He deplored "blockbusting" as much as I did, that deliberate effort by unscrupulous realtors to play on racial fears in order to buy houses from white families at fire sale prices and quickly resell them to blacks at a premium. That was what the Peyton Road barricade was all about. Mayor Allen, with the support of sixteen of the eighteen members of the Board of Aldermen, closed down Peyton Road because it connected a white and black neighborhood where there had been some blockbusting, and the notion was that making the traffic flow more difficult would put an end to it.

Mayor Allen told me later, after we became good friends, that he had consulted with two influential black community leaders beforehand and they agreed with him that the barricade might be a good idea. However, the action created instant anger and antagonism in the black community. It was viewed for what it was, a deliberate act by the city of Atlanta to keep neighborhoods segregated, and the anger was probably more bitter because Mayor Allen was rightly regarded as a progressive leader.

The story received national news coverage and it gave Atlanta, that city proud of its reputation on racial issues, a real black eye. News media from Los Angeles to New York carried it, and some referred to it as Atlanta's version of the Berlin Wall, designed to keep blacks in their place even as the Berlin Wall kept East Germans captive. It was hardly that. It was at first a rather modest barricade of the kind often used to block off part of a street while construction was under way. But it *was* intended to keep blacks from moving into a white neighborhood and thus considered an insult in the black community.

Mayor Allen understood almost right away, I think, that he had made a mistake, but he was a strong, stubborn man, and he hated to give in to pressure. Former Mayor William Hartsfield called him and told him, "As mayor, I made mistakes, but none that could be photographed," like the Peyton Road barricade.

The controversy finally came back to the Board of Aldermen for another vote and the vote was interesting. Only two of the eighteen aldermen at that time were Republicans, Rodney Cook and Richard Freeman, and they were the only two who opposed the Peyton Road barricade. They are both still around, incidentally, Cook a highly successful businessman and Freeman a federal district judge. They both voted against the barricade that second time, but they only picked up one other vote, that of Alderman Buddy Fowlkes, the Georgia Tech track coach who still holds office today on what is now called the Atlanta City Council. Fowlkes simply stood up and said he had voted for the barricade in the hope that it might help stabilize the neighborhoods, but the barricade had created nothing but controversy; it had been a mistake, so now he was changing his vote. I suspect that Mayor Allen and other members of the board agreed with Fowlkes, but were fearful that admitting the mistake and changing their minds would only create a whole new controversy.

Dr. Bell solved that problem—and vented his frustration about the matter—by simply driving right through the barricade, opening up Peyton Road again. Of course he could have been arrested, but the truth of it was that city officials were sick of the controversy. They must have breathed a sigh of relief shortly afterward when a Fulton County Superior Court judge issued an order for the city to take the barricade down and leave it down.

Anyway, Dr. Bell came to see me in anger when he realized that Grady Hospital would examine indigent women on the verge of giving birth only on certain days of the week. It upset me, too, knowing that no woman can control when her baby may arrive. He came to me because we were friends, but also because he knew how active I had been in various causes from the first day I came to Atlanta, that I was not an idle citizen. This was early 1966, after the civil rights laws had passed, and Roy said we ought to protest the Grady policy on the basis that the hospital received a lot of money in federal funds. Indeed, we reviewed federal law as our base, Title VI of the Civil Rights Act of 1964, which barred any racial discrimination in programs financed by such federal funds. I agreed with him entirely, but I said before we started protesting anything we needed to get all the facts.

So we started to put information together. I remember that a fine, intelligent, caring woman named Louise Bradley helped us figure out exactly how much federal money was given to hospitals in the Atlanta area and how little we as black members of the community got in return. Ms. Bradley was with the federal Office of Economic Opportunity (OEO), first assistant to the OEO district supervisor and later promoted to district supervisor for the OEO's southeastern region. There were a lot of things wrong, we found in our investigation, and the treatment of black pregnant women at Grady was just one of them. For one thing, black doctors in Atlanta were not permitted to practice at most hospitals. They were permitted to practice at Hughes Spalding, which was the segregated part of Grady, the black arm of Grady, and at Holy Family Hospital, set up by Catholics and situated in the heart of a black middle-class neighborhood, and that was it.

By this time Dr. Bell had talked to Dr. Otis Smith, a pediatrician, and to my own personal physician, Dr. Albert Davis, who at that time was also president of the NAACP, and to Dr. J. B. Ellison, an internist. Those three, Dr. Bell, and I were the core group who gathered together at my house.

We did get organized, and we put together a lot of basic information: statistical data as to where black doctors could and could not practice, where the barriers were, in what ways black physicians were subjected to insults, all the inconveniences and impositions, any unfairness in medical treatment relating to racial prejudice. We put all this together in a packet of information, and then we invited all sixty-six of the black doctors in Atlanta to come to a meeting so we could make that information available to them. I agreed to be coordinator.

The organization meeting was at the home of Dr. Davis, around his swimming pool, and fully forty of the sixty-six black doctors in Atlanta attended. We thought that was really good, a very high percentage when you consider the kinds of schedules doctors keep and that many already had other commitments. To get almost two-thirds of all the black doctors in Atlanta at the initial session made us feel that we really were getting something started.

I made the presentation, and the doctors all agreed some action should be taken. They asked the core people who had called the meeting to remain in the catalyst role, to be leaders through which everything would be funneled. We decided to organize with a formal name, the Doctors' Committee on Implementation, for no particular reason except that we were resolved that we were going to implement a plan. Dr. J. T. Blasingame, president of the Atlanta Medical Association, became an active *ex officio* member of that committee. Also, we wanted a formal organization because there were a number of doctors who said, "Look, I want to support you but I won't have time to get to many meetings, so let me offer some money now because any organization will have some expenses." I set up a bank account and kept records of everything—the money, copies of letters we sent to members of Congress and other officials, and the dispatches we sent to our own group to let everyone know what was happening.

We wrote officials of the U.S. Department of Health, Education, and Welfare arguing that any use of federal moneys for any medical program that was still segregated was just wrong, and federal law supported that view. We told them we were unhappy about it, but we were also very courteous and asked for advice on how to change the system.

Frankly, it was slow going, and we got the runaround more than once, but we felt sure we would ultimately win. HEW had already issued guidelines saying the public schools could not receive federal funds unless they desegregated. We felt sure that HEW, or if necessary the Congress or the courts, would insist that this same principle applied to federal funds going to any hospital or medical group. Regional offices at the HEW office in Atlanta were sympathetic to us and in effect said they thought we were right, that the hospitals would have to desegregate in order to continue receiving federal funds, but they did not think they could take action unless ordered by Washington.

At one point we held a protest march by black physicians in front of the HEW offices. It was at noon on a Wednesday, since that was the afternoon most doctors closed their offices. It got good media coverage because it was an unusual demonstration, all black doctors, who are not typically the people marching anywhere in protest. Dr. King and the Rev. Abernathy knew what we were doing and encouraged us; both said they would come march with us or have a rally or whatever seemed appropriate.

We were getting some response, but this process dragged on for months and months. I began telling the doctors that it was too slow, that we needed to go to Washington and talk to people firsthand. My doctors were a little reluctant to give up that much of their time, but the leaders of the group said they would go. What pushed us was that we had finally gotten HEW to set a deadline for eighteen Atlanta area hospitals — July 1, 1966. The deadline was plain; these hospitals had to desegregate by that date or lose federal funding. Well, the people running the hospitals did not really want to do either one, desegregate or give up the money, so several of the major hospitals applied for an extension. HEW approved it, extending that July 1 date to September 15. That was when we finally went to Washington, in late August.

We had really done our homework. We had the list of the hospitals and exactly how much federal money each received, how many patients each treated, whether they treated white and black patients, how many doctors white and black were admitted to practice at each hospital, just every possible breakdown of information so that nobody could pretend we did not have a good, conclusive case. We went to Washington the night before our scheduled appointments the next day with Senator Edward Kennedy, who was encouraging, and Georgia Senator Herman Talmadge, who was not, and also with officials with the U.S. Public Health Service, who were evasive. We met also with New York Senator Jacob Javits, who offered encouragement.

Our research was thorough. It was plain what the law said. Title VI of the Civil Rights Act of 1964 stated, "No person in the United States shall, on the ground of race, color, or national origin, be excluded from participation in, be denied the benefits of, or be subjected to discrimination under any program or activity receiving federal financial assistance." Moreover, the American Hospital Association asked HEW officials to answer certain questions relating to hospitals, so that there could be no doubt what the law required. The answers to these questions were reviewed by HEW Secretary John W. Gardner and Surgeon General William H. Stewart and then distributed to hospital administrators over the country. Hospital discrimination exists, one answer read, "when a patient, visitor, professional staff member, or trainee is treated differently solely because of his race, color, or national origin. Compliance with Title VI, in brief, involves admission policies, patient room assignments, availability of services and facilities, staff privileges, and training programs." Another directive relating to hospital compliance said that if a hospital "does not comply with the provisions of Title VI, it will not receive funds under Medicare and will not be able to apply for grants under other federal programs." How could it be stated more clearly? Yet we still encountered resistance.

One U.S. Public Health official gave us a hard time after we presented our information to him, all the data about the Atlanta hospitals, saying that our materials were not really helpful on these matters because he would have to check the department's own records. We said fine, we would like to review his records too. That was when he went really evasive on us. We had all been making polite conversation at the beginning of the meeting, the way you do to get to know someone, and we had said that we only planned to be in Washington for the rest of the day and intended to fly back to Atlanta that evening. Wouldn't you know, this official insisted that all the pertinent records were in a building in Baltimore and there would not be time for him to get them for us to review since we were only going to be there for the day. I usually let the doctors do all the talking, but this time I interrupted and said to the official that we would stay in Washington as long as it would take to get those records produced.

That made him really fidgety and the doctors too, some, because they all had appointments the next day. But I told them later that I was prepared to stay over even if they had to go back to Atlanta that evening; I felt sure that just one of us staying would be enough of a threat to get at those records. So then the official changed his tune and said he would try to get the records over to his office by four that afternoon.

We went to Senator Talmadge's office from there. He was most difficult for us because he is so clever. I doubt if he ever went to a meeting without being completely prepared, and he knew exactly who we were and why we were there and what we were trying to do. He said he could not meet with us long because he had another meeting, so I started by saying that our small group of black doctors had a presentation to make, and we felt sure he would want to know if there were injustice being committed in his own home state.

We had scripted our presentation almost like a play, starting with a modest opening and then building up. Dr. Albert Davis was the suave, smooth member of the group, and he would make a presentation in an intellectual way, very low key, saying, "Senator, we think we have a problem in Atlanta and we want your help." Then would come Dr. J. B. Ellison who would have a tone of slight irritation in his voice: "Now, Senator, I don't think you really heard what Dr. Davis was saying." And if that didn't work, Dr. Otis Smith was the one who would begin to get tough, saying, "Now, Senator, the reason you didn't hear what Dr. Davis was saying was because you really did not want to hear." Finally, Dr. Bell was our clean-up hitter, and, assuming we had not gotten any helpful response at all, he would strike a truly fierce note, practically threatening to go get a stick and hit somebody over the head, or worse, to call in the Black Power militants.

The senator kept trying to joke about it, saying he had not had time to look at any medical records. He said he had talked to doctors before but had never practiced any medicine, so he really didn't know what doctors had to go through. It was as if he were half-trying to be funny but also insisting, well, he just didn't understand all this. One of my doctors said, "Senator, what Dr. Davis was trying to tell you is that a poor black woman has to have labor pains on a certain day of the week, that she can't have labor pains on just any day and get any help at Grady Hospital." And Talmadge said, "Well, doctor, I don't know a lot about labor pains because I never personally had any children; I always left that to my wife." He laughed out loud when he said this, as if it were all a great big joke.

Dr. Smith waded in and said, "Senator, you may not practice any medicine but I understand you practice a little law, and you ought to be able to understand that we have a human concern here. You can hear what we are trying to tell you, and we have got the data, the statistics, right here so that you can read it for yourself." Talmadge said finally that he had to read an awful lot of material relating to legislation but that if we would leave our information he would try to read it. Dr. Bell erupted at this point and made mention of Senator Talmadge's father, the late Governor Eugene Talmadge, who had been a strong segregationist throughout his political career. "Your daddy didn't do right," Dr. Bell said, "and you don't want to do right."

Talmadge was impervious to all the pressures we were trying to put on him, and he said again that he had to leave for his other meeting, so I made one more effort at summing up.

"Senator," I said, "you have not practiced any medicine and your practice of law apparently did not help you understand what these doctors have tried to tell you. You say you don't have much time to read but let me ask you this—can't you hear my words?" I summed up what the doctors had been saying, then I noted Dr. Bell's assertion, based on history, that the Talmadges had never done right. "I don't want to deal in *never*," I told him, and I said that somehow I believed the senator was an honorable man, and I believed he would hear the voices of the women who could not time their labor pains for a particular day and yet nevertheless deserved the same care in labor and delivery as the women in the senator's family had received, and that since no woman knows exactly when she will give birth she ought to have at least the freedom of mind to know she will have a healthy hospital and the chance of a normal birth, even if she does not happen to be white.

"Surely, Senator," I said, "you can hear that? I hope you can hear what these women are saying, Senator," I concluded, "because they need somebody with your degree of humanitarian concern and your good will to try to get something done about this problem."

An aide to Senator Talmadge called me several days later and said that the senator had been impressed with our presentation and would try to help. I believed that I had established a friendship, and it later proved true.

Some time afterward, when I took my little nephew from Los Angeles to Washington, Senator Talmadge treated us to lunch in the Senate Dining Room where we sampled that famous bean soup. He always made himself available whenever I called him on the telephone. Later, when I remarried in 1974, the senator sent me a lovely wedding present.

That day the black doctors and I went back to our hotel, the Washington Hilton, feeling that things were going reasonably well, in that, however reluctantly, the Public Health Service official had finally promised to produce their records for us to review and Senator Talmadge had at least said he would read the information we had brought him. "Gentlemen," I said after we got back, "we have been seeing all these officials, but what we really need to do is go see the president." I was probably just talking big, and my guys told me I had finally gone crazy, but then I started getting serious about it. Come to think of it, I told them, we had written President Johnson a letter, and I resented the fact that he had never responded. "Let me call the White House," I said, "and find out why he has not given us the courtesy of a reply. In fact," I said, "I'm going to tell them now that we don't want a letter; since we are in Washington we would like a personal visit with President Johnson."

My friends thought now I had really lost my mind, but we were all sitting in a hotel suite together and they listened carefully as I called the White House and asked to speak to the president. Of course I did not get the president on the telephone just like that, but I got *somebody* and I explained who we were and where we were staying and how we had written the president on a certain date (I had the exact date because I had my files with me). I said that we had written to explain that blacks were suffering in Atlanta only because they were black, that if it were not for the segregated system these people would be getting responsible health care and black doctors would be freely moving and practicing in hospitals chosen by their patients. President Johnson talked about being a decent president, I said, and building a Great Society, and yet he did not even have the courtesy to answer our letter about such matters.

"You can talk about having a Great Society," I told this White House staffer, "but we can't have a Great Society when black people suffer a lack of decent medical care *because* they are black and the president is still allowing federal money to go to these segregated hospitals. So I want to know," I said, "is the president insensitive to these matters?" We were planning a press conference for ten o'clock the next morning, I said, and we wanted to visit with the president before that press conference, but in any case we would not leave Washington until we met with President Johnson.

So I hung up the telephone, and then all of us simply broke up. It was a good laugh, frankly, none of us thinking anything would come from the telephone call but feeling good that we had at least registered our protest that President Johnson had not bothered to answer our letter.

Since we probably would not hear from the U.S. Public Health Service office until four o'clock or later and it would be a hassle to check out of the hotel that late and catch a plane, we all decided to stay over. Two of the doctors had attended Howard University Medical School in Washington and knew the city well, so that was part of our decision, too, since they would be able to pick some good restaurant where we would all have dinner. It was early afternoon by this time, maybe around three o'clock, and we were all excited and keyed up from the day's activities, but we had completed our scheduled appointments. We doubted if even the Public Health Service would call that afternoon, let alone the White House. I had taken off my high heels and changed into a lounging outfit, thinking that our work was done and our biggest decision left was where we were going to dinner. Dr. Bell said he was going downstairs for a drink in the hotel bar and to let him know when we decided where we wanted to go for dinner.

We were talking about restaurants when the telephone rang.

I assumed the call might be from the Public Health official, so the first thing the voice on the telephone said was confusing: "Is this Doctor Clayton?" I said, no, I was Ms. Clayton, not a doctor, but I was with a delegation of doctors from Atlanta, and who was calling? The White House was calling, the voice said, and President Johnson wanted to meet with our delegation at four o'clock. They needed to verify the names of the doctors in the group and wanted to tell me where to come and at what White House entrance we would be expected. I gave the names and wrote down the instructions and said, yes, we could be there at four. My group was looking at me, stunned, when I hung up the telephone, and I guess we were all thinking how we had been laughing hysterically only a short while before at the very idea that the president might see us. I was very calm and cool and collected on the telephone, and I remember one of the doctors looked at me and said, "My gosh, you sounded as if you really expected the White House to call."

It was almost three-thirty by this time and we had to hurry if we were going to get to the White House by four. I had to change clothes again, and I asked one of the doctors to go downstairs and find Dr. Bell, because Roy had said he might go visit an old friend. In fact, Dr. Bell almost missed our White House visit. He had just called his friend and then tried to call the suite to let us know he was going out, but he had gotten a busy signal and had left a message for us with the bartender. He was heading out the door when we caught up with him and explained we were on our way to the White House.

As we all piled into a taxi, the doctors kept telling me how nervous and excited they were, how they had never been to the White House before, and I kept telling them to be calm and act as if they had been to the White House dozens of times. The security people had our names at the gate, and we started walking up that curving driveway from Pennsylvania Avenue. All of a sudden it hit me. I stopped in my tracks and said, "Oh my gosh, this really is the White House!" They all burst out laughing because I had been working so hard to keep them calm and now that we were actually there I was the one getting excited.

We met first with Douglas Cater, a special assistant to President Johnson, who said the president was tied up with other matters but wanted Mr. Cater to meet with us until he was free. He said the president wanted to apologize for not responding to our letter and for any inconvenience that had caused us. The president intended to get personally involved to help remedy our concerns, he said, and he wanted to know if we had any further information to leave, in addition to what we had sent in our letter, so we gave him the most updated data we had. I remember Mr. Cater's words: "We do not condone segregation in any medical facility receiving federal funds, and we will do something about it."

The biggest thrill was that President Johnson did come in to speak to us, if only for a few moments, and he said he had wanted to meet us and that he shared our concerns. He wanted to be sure that Mr. Cater had gotten all the information we wanted to give him.

Even though our threat to have a news conference had been just that—a threat—it turned out we did have one. Dr. Bell left our meeting before it was over and alerted the White House press people that we were there and would answer questions after we left the president. There were a lot of microphones and a lot of media coverage—as much, according to some of the press, as they had ever seen for a private group. That is, we did not represent any national organization or foreign country or major union. We were a small group of private citizens who had organized a committee to protest one specific injustice.

The media coverage of that news conference went all over the country. The *Atlanta Constitution* ran a wire story account quoting our group as accusing the federal government of "backing off" from enforcing desegregation guidelines upon Emory University Hospital. Only one of the eighteen hospitals we had surveyed, we said, was actually in compliance with the guidelines while others had desegregated "on paper" only. I was quoted as saying that Emory was "key to the whole problem" because it controlled five hospitals, and it almost seemed that HEW and the federal government were "fearful of Emory."

Now, let me explain that Emory today is a marvelous institution and has changed a great deal in the twenty-plus years since that news conference. But we focused on Emory at that time for several good reasons. Emory had an important medical school, affiliations with five different hospitals, including Grady, and received more federal moneys than any other medical facility in the region. In fact, at that time Emory had recently received more than $5 million in federal money for medical research, so Emory really *was* the key to getting some changes made.

Our doctors' committee acquired new credibility back in Atlanta because of this national news coverage.

We ended up that same summer holding a regional conference in Atlanta, inviting black doctors from over the South. Close to one hundred black physicians from eight southern states met in Atlanta for an unprecedented one-day conference to air their grievances with HEW officials over continuing discrimination in southern hospitals, in direct violation of the 1964 Civil Rights Act. Dr. Leonidas Berry of Chicago, president of the National Medical Association, offered a different dimension, asserting that hospitals in Chicago and other northern cities were just as guilty as southern hospitals in their discriminatory practices. Washington officials attending the conference included Dr. Leo Gherig, Deputy Surgeon General; N. J. Labassi, HEW legal counsel; Robert J. Nash, HEW chief compliance officer; and Sherrie Arnstein, Assistant to the Secretary of HEW.

It still took time, several more months of pressuring the federal government to press the desegregation guidelines, but the hospitals finally complied so that black patients and physicians had free and equal access to almost all hospitals in Atlanta and Georgia and across the South.

We were impatient then, my doctors and I, because it seemed to take so long, but probably in the historical context it was not long for such significant changes to take place. Perhaps one year passed from the time we started talking about the issue until those changes occurred. By the way, this project was the inspiration behind a national movement to desegregate hospitals all around the country. The Doctor's Committee on Implementation was honored for its courageous efforts by the National Medical Association at its annual convention.

Xernona with Dr. Otis Smith and Dr. Albert Davis, leaders of the Doctors' Committee on Implementation.

Xernona with Linda Dorian, executive director of the National Association of Business and Professional Women.

Xernona and husband Paul Brady, autographing his book.

Xernona with husband Paul and his children, Paul, Jr., and Laura.

Dr. Mary Lee Brady, Paul's former wife, with Xernona.

Former mayor Sam Massell, former WAGA general manager "Buddy" Ray, Xernona, Mrs. Ray, and J. Lowell Ware, publisher of the Atlanta Voice.

Senator Herman Talmadge and Xernona.

Xernona greeted at the White House by President Jimmy Carter; looking on is California senator Diane Watson.

Chicago attorney Tom Todd, Dollars & Sense executive Nina Tabb, Minister Louis Farrakhan, Xernona, and Mrs. Farrakhan.

184

Ted Turner welcomes Xernona to Moscow following her detainment in Amsterdam.

National Sickle Cell president Dr. Charles Whitten and Xernona pose with President Bush and 1989 Sickle Cell Poster Children Anthony Wayne Smith and Lori Beth Bonnell.

Tom Teepen, editorial page editor of the Atlanta Constitution, *Xernona, Anheuser-Bush Vice President Wayne Smith, III, and Dr. Maurice Dawkins, civil rights activist.*

William Shaw, TBS Vice President of Administration, Xernona, actor Louis Gossett, Jr., and Seattle mayor Norman B. Rice at the Goodwill Games in Seattle.

Xernona, CNN News anchor Bernard Shaw, and former CNN News anchor Pat Harvey, now news anchor at KCAL, Los Angeles.

Xernona with her administrative assistant, Gioconda Miller.

Jasvinder S. Sidhu, 1987
East Lansing, Michigan

Debra R. Jones, 1988
Flint, Michigan

Duonne Martin, 1989
Alton, Illinois

Angela C. Dabney, 1990
Albuquerque, New Mexico

Recipients of the Xernona Clayton
Scholarship, awarded by the American
Intercultural Student Exchange.

Tarik A. O. Ali, 1991
Atlanta, Georgia

188

Eighteen

My recess from television did not last too long. Yet I never imagined when I first became involved with Turner Broadcasting that I would be part of an effort to take over the CBS television network, or participate in the Goodwill Games in Moscow, or even explore the possibility that Ted Turner might run for president of the United States.

Ted has often been considered controversial; he's been called everything from "Captain Courageous" to "the Mouth of the South," and many have deemed him arrogant and likely to self-destruct in his overly ambitious ventures. But he has confounded his critics; Turner Broadcasting is one of the success stories of our time, and CNN has become the single most influential news organization in the world, often monitored by leaders of nations around the globe.

I always remember the first time I ever saw Ted Turner in person, long before I worked for him. It was at a banquet given by the Atlanta Urban League to honor two people: Ted because he had hired Bill Lucas as general manager of the Atlanta Braves, the first black general manager in major-league baseball, and Heman Sweatt who made headlines several years before when he became the first black to attend the

University of Texas law school. Both men were being honored that night for their human rights efforts.

Sweatt spoke first, and it was clear that he was very moved at receiving the award. He started to talk in some detail about how difficult his experience had been. He wanted to attend his state's law school but was denied admission because he was black. It took Thurgood Marshall, before he was named to the U.S. Supreme Court, and the NAACP, and practically an act of God to get him in. It was difficult and painful for him, and he told us that night how shattering the experience had been, even though he felt quite determined.

He was a short man, only a little over five feet tall, and he told us how frustrated and angry he was when the law school denied him admission and how those vitriolic tones must have been in his voice when he went to see Thurgood Marshall. Marshall frowned and told him, "Well, Heman, the first thing we have got to do is deal with reality. You are not a very big fellow, and with your size your anger will not *scare* anybody. So you have to get over being angry, and we will just have to sit down and think out what we can do in a legal way." Marshall was completely good-natured in all this, Sweatt recounted, and it became a humorous point between them that Marshall would tease him whenever Sweatt's anger got the best of him.

Sweatt went on to talk about how difficult it seemed, when all he wanted was to get a good education, when he had the money to go and the will to go, and the only thing keeping him from the law school of his home state was that his skin was black. He found this so hard, he said, because there is nothing you can do about your skin, nothing; you can't change it . . . and yet here he was put in a certain category because of race, barred from opportunity because of this purely accidental factor. He told us, too, how he had thought the big step would be just getting admitted, that all would go well with him then, but he found out differently. Staying in the law school proved to be the hardest thing of all, because other students would spit on him and insult him. It was a very moving account, and everyone at the dinner applauded this man mightily because of his commitment, courage, and determination.

Ted was clearly moved, too, and he was all choked up, even tearful, when he got up to receive his award. He felt almost like rejecting his own award, he said, because he felt unworthy to stand on the same stage with a man like Heman Sweatt. "All I did," I remember Ted saying, "was to hire a man because it was the right thing to do and you are going to give me an award, and yet here is another man who has been through such incredible and difficult experiences over a period of years." Everyone there felt Ted's sincerity, and he mesmerized that audience. He did accept the award, and of course he deserved it. Maybe he saw naming Bill Lucas as the first black general manager in major-league baseball as a simple thing, making a decision because it was the right thing to do, but all of big-league baseball had thus far failed to make such a decision, and it was the breaking of a significant barrier. In fact, Hall of Famer Hank Aaron, Atlanta Braves' vice president, has been recently critical of baseball's continued failure to offer greater opportunities for minorities. Conditions for blacks have not improved much, said Aaron, in the four years since the Dodgers' Al Campanis made his infamous statement that blacks may not have "the necessities" for front-office position in baseball.

So I gained a respect at the dinner that night for a man named Ted Turner, a man I did not really know, a man who had had a lot of controversial things written about him and yet who came across that evening as a quite different kind of person, as a person of great conviction and human compassion, one capable of truly understanding the painful ordeal of Heman Sweatt.

In 1979 I went to work for what later came to be known as Ted's SuperStation, WTBS, though it was then only a low-power station which ran mostly old movies. Station manager

Sid Pike called me at the prompting of my friend Dee Woods, then secretary to Ted Turner, and asked if I would suggest some ideas for local programming, and I did that part-time for a while. (Sid is now president of CNN International and Special Projects and Dee has become vice president/assistant to the chairman — Ted Turner.) One of the first programs we produced was called "Sweet Auburn," which was the long-time nickname for Auburn Avenue in Atlanta, a street with a marvelous history, including a reputation at one time as being the richest black street in America. Its early residents included black professionals and business people and a lot of "firsts," like the nation's first black radio station, the first black daily newspaper, one of the first black insurance companies, and one of the first black savings and loan institutions. We did a documentary on that rich history, and the program won an Emmy award for the station.

I was working with the program director and the local producers and never actually encountered Ted Turner for a long time. I was coming in only part-time, and he was rarely there because he was busy putting CNN and Turner Broadcasting System together. I am an early morning person, and I was at the station at 6:30 a.m. one day starting to work on a program we had scheduled. Now, I knew Mr. Turner occasionally spent the night in his office; I had heard his big office on the third floor had the kind of couch that converted into a bed and that he sometimes stayed over when he had been to a Braves game or had an early morning appointment. I also knew that he occasionally wandered down to the commissary early in the morning to get a cup of coffee. That was on my floor, at the far end of the building from his office.

On this one particular morning I came out of my office and ran into Ted Turner, who was wearing a great broad white towel and apparently nothing else. "What are you doing here so early?" he asked, and I told him I came in early all the time. He was in his bare feet with the towel wrapped around him and said, "I hate to walk down to the commissary for coffee. Is it possible that you have coffee?" I said yes, I had just made a fresh pot in my office, and he asked rather diffidently if he could have a cup. I said yes, of course, and we chatted for a moment, and he got his coffee and went back upstairs.

He came down again the next day for another cup of coffee, and that was the beginning of our regular morning coffee klatch. I love good conversation, and we talked about almost everything. I would often disagree with some point he would make, and he seemed to like that, as long as I could give a good reason, a real argument. I did not know it at the time but he was weighing what I call my *thinkability*. Ted is almost intimidating because he is not just smart but knowledgeable about a wide range of subjects. I was a music major in school, but his knowledge of music, of musicians and composers, easily matched mine. I had grown up in the church and attended Sunday School regularly, so I thought I knew a little something about the Bible, but I found that Ted had read the Bible straight through more than once and knew much more than I did. We would talk about the Bible, race relations, global concerns, current issues — everything. I am a voracious reader, and I usually read the newspaper early in the morning, and sometimes he would just ask, "What's in the paper?" and we would talk about whatever was going on in the world.

It may sound unorthodox to have coffee with the boss when he is only wearing a towel, but it was all perfectly proper. Ted was considerably more covered up with that towel than some people I see in bathing suits or shorts. But that towel *did* give me concern once. Ted asked me one morning to give my opinion of a video tape on the VCR in his office, so we proceeded up the stairs to the third floor. There was a door to be opened at the top of the stairs, and I could see Ted struggling to do the gentlemanly thing and open the door for me, but he had his hot coffee in one hand and was holding the towel with the other. He was not going to give up his coffee, was my thought, and I was concerned that he might let the towel go with the other hand in order to open that door, so I quickly stepped in front of him, said thank you very much, and opened the door for him.

Ted began asking me to view programs and give him an opinion. People often would simply send in tapes and ask Ted to fund them, and he would ask my opinion as to whether they were worth funding. For example, it might be a public affairs program, and he would ask if I thought we could find a commercial sponsor for it. Or he might ask if a particular program would be offensive to minorities, or to women, or to people sensitive to environmental issues. I came to realize that he truly did respect my opinion. Several people reported to me that he liked the way I always backed up my views with a reason. He had no obligation, obviously, to honor my recommendations, but I understand that many times he did.

I learned as I got to know him better that he greatly valued punctuality. He was a prompt and punctual person himself, and he respected people who did whatever they were supposed to do on time. I always felt that way, too, no doubt in part because of what my father had always told me about keeping one's obligations, about doing what you said you would do — even if it were just to meet on the street corner the next day at noon in order to count cars.

It happened that I had to fire a secretary one time because she was late coming to work repeatedly. I felt that while I could not control everybody else's habits I could certainly control my own staff. I gave this secretary plenty of warning and fired her only after she failed again and again to mend her ways. Even so, she resented her firing and decided to complain directly to Mr. Turner. Turner had a regular parking space at the television station, and she waited there for him to park one day and then started telling him as he walked to the building what a terrible manager I was, how unfair and mean I had been to fire her for being just a few minutes late, and how he should get rid of me. Someone who observed all this told me later that he never stopped walking, never broke stride, just responded by saying, "That gives her a high rating in my book if she fired you for tardiness."

My career with Turner Broadcasting has been an exciting one, even if I sometimes think I am one of Ted Turner's favorite utility infielders. I first worked part-time at WTBS helping produce documentaries, then for a time in the early 1980s hosting their weekly public affairs show. Then, in sequence, I became coordinator of minority affairs for Turner Broadcasting, director of public affairs for WTBS, vice president for public affairs for WTBS, and in 1988 became the assistant corporate vice president for urban affairs for the Turner Broadcasting System. That last title translates into acting as liaison for Turner to civic and minority groups in Atlanta and around the country and, as a practical matter, it means getting involved in all manner of special projects and programs. I truly appreciate the help and support I received from Linda Hollingsworth, who preceded me as public affairs director at WTBS, and from Jim Kitchell, WTBS Station Manager after Sid Pike. Bill Shaw, now Vice President of Administration for Turner Broadcasting, has been extremely supportive on any number of programs and projects. In his previous position as Vice President of Personnel, he was strong in his zeal to make equal employment for minorities a reality at Turner Broadcasting.

Some projects have been particularly intriguing, like being involved in the Turner Broadcasting effort to take over the Columbia Broadcasting System, or participating in the Goodwill Games in Moscow, and even once going around the country to talk to people about the possibility of Ted Turner running for president of the United States.

When Ted decided on tackling CBS, in 1985, he asked me to be part of the small group of perhaps eight or ten people at the strategy sessions. It became a national, even international, story in the communications field, and I felt truly flattered that he wanted me to be part of such an important task as the takeover effort. He valued my opinion, I knew, yet I had no expertise in high finance or corporate mergers, so I worked very hard to become informed on such matters and tried to make a contribution. Being an avid reader, I was knowledgeable on industry issues generally. I had done my own television programs, had carefully observed what the networks were doing, and had contacts with people all over the country, so I thought I brought to those meetings a strong overall understanding of the television industry. Nonetheless, I worked very hard and consider that effort perhaps the most delicate and challenging assignment I ever had, in a category separate from anything else I ever did.

Turner's attempted takeover of CBS was reported at great length, and I don't think this book is a place for a blow-by-blow account. Two things do stand out in my mind, however. First, CBS and the television industry in general discounted the takeover altogether at first, believing apparently that Ted Turner was some kind of maverick outside the real business world, not to be taken seriously. It is true that Ted is easy to underestimate because he seems so unorthodox, but that proved a very mistaken judgment on the part of CBS. Second, that takeover effort became a serious matter indeed. We surprised the industry and we thought we came very close to making it work. It was certainly clear, though, that CBS underestimated the resources Ted could muster, that they did not regard him as a real threat at first. The CBS people first felt they could just waltz around it, I think, without really worrying about a takeover by anybody, let alone Ted Turner. In the end, CBS had to take dramatic steps to avoid the takeover, steps that proved so financially costly that the company eventually had to make substantial personnel cuts to recoup its losses. The fact that Turner Broadcasting even came close to taking over one of the existing major networks changed the way people thought about the industry.

Ted really is easy to underestimate. I remember how the American Broadcasting Company viewed him as an easy target in the early 1980s. The basic CNN programming had been put in place and then came Headline News, a separate service offered to cable companies. ABC decided to begin a rival headline service for cable, apparently deciding that Ted had hit on something worthwhile and also assuming that their long-established network news operation could easily create a headline news product that would overwhelm CNN's. The competitive outcome was just the reverse, CNN the clear winner, with ABC giving up its effort after some millions of dollars in losses.

. . .

The Goodwill Games were planned by Ted and Turner Broadcasting as something similar to the Olympics, yet with the ultimate emphasis on the good will that can come from international sports when all political concerns are excluded. It was a great coup to persuade the Soviet Union to host those Goodwill Games in 1986.

Ted wanted CNN to be represented in Moscow by a delegation that included *all* Americans, and he asked me to invite a minority delegation. It was an expensive trip, probably about $3,500 per person for the few days in Moscow, and at Ted's urging I put together a minority list of about twenty-five people who were invited to be part of the CNN delegation with all their expenses paid. We ended up, I recall, with twenty-seven people altogether.

There were a lot of things to be done for the group, from extending the initial invitations to disseminating all the necessary information: the schedule for the Goodwill Games, what to wear that time of year in Moscow, information about the Soviet Union, its history and language and culture. I also worked on their passport and visa needs and all their flight schedules, a complicated task considering that these people were coming from all over the United States, East Coast and West Coast, and all needed to arrive in Amsterdam at about the same time. Amsterdam was the point of rendezvous, with people coming from all directions and then gathering for a luncheon before flying on to Moscow. We had a sightseeing tour of Amsterdam planned for that afternoon and then were to depart for the Soviet Union at about five o'clock.

Members of my delegation were full of praise for my efforts at helping them plan and make their arrangements, but the crazy and ironic thing was that I had looked after them so well that I had not looked after myself enough! We were handling visas for people in the party through an office at CNN, and they came trickling in over a period of time. I was traveling with my husband, Judge Paul Brady, and his visa came in on time but mine, alas, did not. I remember TBS Vice President Bob Wussler telling me, as we departed the Atlanta airport, not to worry, that they would somehow get the visa to me in Amsterdam.

A host of the Goodwill Games met us in Amsterdam to take care of details, directing us to our hotel rooms and later to the luncheon, and he was supposed to have my visa. Not so, I discovered, but the host was very reassuring. Someone was working on it, he said, and I should plan to keep to the schedule, send my luggage to the airport and go on the afternoon sightseeing tour, and the visa would be waiting for me at the airport.

Not so again. I would have to remain in Amsterdam, I was told, because I simply would not be allowed into the Soviet Union without the visa. Probably only overnight. Surely the visa would arrive by the next morning and I could come on the next available flight. My husband wanted to stay with me, but he was told that Soviet officials were strict in not permitting any changes in travel plans. So, almost unbelievingly, I watched my husband and my delegation and my luggage depart for Moscow while I remained behind in Amsterdam where I did not know one single living soul.

It was almost funny. I was wearing a suit that I was really planning to discard due to its age and condition, but I had decided to get one more good wear out of it. Luckily, it was the kind that didn't wrinkle because my visa did not come the next day and the one day's delay turned into four days. I wore that suit every day, washing the blouse out carefully each night.

It turned out I had some company. I was the only member of my delegation whose visa had not come through, but back at the hotel I found two CNN staff members, Ken Christiansen and Tom Todd, whose visas had also been delayed and who were also waiting for some word. We speculated as to whether there could be some special reason why *our* visas were being held up. One of the men had once been in the Federal Bureau of Investigation, and the other's father had worked for the Central Intelligence Agency, so we thought that might explain it. I had been active in the civil rights movement, but we thought surely that would have seemed a plus to a Soviet official. I had also been a visitor to Israel several years before as a guest of the government, and I wondered if that could have been the reason.

The long delay was a great disappointment at the time because I had done so much planning for my delegation and I felt somehow I was not fulfilling my mission. And although I was in a good hotel, the Amsterdam Hilton, I started getting cabin fever almost at once because I was spending much of my time in my room waiting for some word of my visa. The frustration was even greater because it was so hard to telephone and contact any of my group in Moscow. You could place a call but there might be a four-hour wait. Bob Wussler instructed his administrative assistant, Debbie Monger, to make his "hotline" telephone in Moscow available to my hauband Paul, which reduced that waiting time. I finally called my sister in Los Angeles to tell her of my plight, how I was almost climbing the walls of my room, and she responded in the nicest way. She called family and friends all over the United States and gave them my number in the hotel in Amsterdam. She got a regular calling caravan going, and I caught up on all the news. It was a wonderful connection with a world I knew better than the one I was now in.

The Goodwill Games program for my group lasted for only one week, so when I finally got my visa on the fifth day, I had missed all but the last two days in Moscow. Yet my arrival was a great moment because my group had told everyone about "the woman stranded in Amsterdam," so the people there treated me like a celebrity. Bob Wussler, then Turner's Executive Vice President, sent his limousine to meet me at the airport and arranged a welcome breakfast the next morning. Mr. Wussler even made special arrangements for my husband and me to stay over in Moscow a few extra days if we wished, but I decided to return to Amsterdam and the United States with my group. I did not want to lose my delegation again!

Ted is a fearless warrior who, paradoxically, wants above all to be an ambassador for peace. The Goodwill Games in Moscow represented one keystone of his energetic efforts to promote global understanding. He was honored for those efforts in March of 1990 with an award from the Volunteers of America in Los Angeles, an award presented in conjunction with the Soviet Embassy in that city and *Soviet Life* magazine.

• • •

Ted Turner gave serious thought to the possibility of running for president of the United States in the early 1980s, and I first heard him mention the idea at one of our morning coffee klatches. He was often critical of what was happening in our world, how there were not enough human rights, not enough love. He would talk about people not loving each other, people not treating each other with decency, not having respect for flag and country and family values. A president could do more to emphasize such values, he said, and we would have a good country, a better country. Ted seemed completely sincere and idealistic when voicing these concerns, and then one morning he said, "I believe I could do that." I didn't understand what he meant at first, thinking he was still talking philosophically about our nation's values, but he finally asked quite directly and seriously, "Xernona, do you think I could become president of the United States?"

I thought about it seriously for a moment, and then I told him, "No, Ted, I don't think you could." This answer shocked him, but, characteristically, he wanted me to back up my opinion.

I told him that I thought the perception of the public was that he was a playboy, not serious enough. Stories in the media had portrayed him as irresponsible. I thought I knew better than that, personally, because I saw Ted tending to business at the SuperStation and CNN and I knew that Turner Broadcasting was incredibly successful. People were already beginning to say that Ted was revolutionizing the entire television industry, and yet as a presidential candidate I felt that he would have a controversial public perception to overcome.

Anyway, he asked me to take the idea seriously with him and help him explore the possibility. It became a serious project. I contacted people over the country, in politics, government, and business, to get their reactions. I remember talking to Hamilton Jordan, who managed Jimmy Carter's successful campaign for the White House in 1976, and I mention his name because he is a friend and I am sure he will not mind. I don't feel free to mention other names because these conversations generally were conducted with a pledge of absolute confidentiality.

I found, however, three prevailing opinions about Ted's presidential prospects. First, many echoed my observation that Ted would have to overcome something of a playboy image in order to be taken seriously as a presidential candidate. But, second, that his enormous success with the Super-Station and CNN would be considered a great plus. Also, third, Ted's reputation as an independent spirit, a maverick, a man who had successfully bucked the conventional wisdom in the TV industry, could indeed help him become a very serious White House candidate.

I honestly do not know if Ted still has political ambitions for the White House, even in the back of his mind. But I do know this. He would be a caring, intelligent, capable candidate. I believe he would be a good president.

Nineteen

That a determined individual can take something evil and turn it into something good is a notion my father drilled into me as I was growing up, and I have often found it true in my own life. But it was the last thing in my mind when I got a routine invitation to speak to a women's group in Rome, Georgia. I say routine because I do get a lot of invitations to speak and I accept as many as I can. I often represent Turner Broadcasting at events, and sometimes Ted Turner will ask me personally to attend a function that he thinks important but can't manage to attend himself.

Yet the invitation to speak in Rome was more than routine, too. It was from Rome's Business and Professional Women's Club, and I valued speaking to such women's groups because I believed I had something so say to them, sharing my experiences in the civil rights movement and comparing them to discrimination against women in the marketplace. Also, I thought of Rome as a progressive city, in part because I had heard a lot about Berry College there, a small coeducational college whose 1,600-plus students come from all over the United States as well as from overseas. *U.S. News and World Report* once described Berry as one of the best small colleges in the country with an incredible campus of 28,000 beautiful acres, acknowledged to be the world's largest.

I also had come to know something about Rome's history because after I moved to Georgia in the mid-1960s to work for Dr. King I tried to read as much as I could about the history of my new state. How Rome came to be founded made an interesting story.

At a spring near the junction where the Etowah and the Oostanaula rivers meet to form the mighty Coosa River, two weary travelers stopped to rest one day in 1834. They fell into conversation with a third wayfarer, a planter, and as they looked around them they began talking about how the site would be ideal for a future trading center. There was abundant water, a heavy growth of timber, and obviously fertile soil. The three men recruited two other friends to join them in developing plans for the new community. They obtained ferry rights for the rivers, drew plans for streets and land lots and public buildings, and then asked the state legislature to designate the area as Floyd County, with the new trading center to become the county seat.

A city thus was born, located approximately ninety miles northwest of Atlanta, and all that was lacking was a name. The five men who had done the planning decided that one of them should have the honor of naming the new city, and, rather than argue or debate about it, they all wrote their suggestions on slips of paper and dropped them in a hat. The name drawn out was Rome, conceived because of the similarity of the hills around the new city to the seven hills of ancient Rome in Italy.

Rome, Georgia, was formally incorporated as a city in 1847 and prospered as a trading hub until the Civil War, when most of its young men answered the call to arms. The city itself fell victim, too, to General Sherman's March to the Sea. Another great *Atlanta Constitution* editor, Henry Grady, made a speech after the war to an audience that included General Sherman. Sherman was much admired in the South as a distinguished soldier, Grady alleged, but was believed to be a little careless with fire.

Anyway, I knew that this community of Rome had rebuilt after the Civil War to become again the trading hub and also the educational, cultural, and religious center of northwest Georgia.

The first word I got of the invitation to speak to the Business and Professional Women's Club in Rome was from a woman named Amy Pimper, a stockbroker, who told me she was on their program committee and wanted to know if I would consider speaking to their annual dinner at the end of April. This was a tentative invitation, she explained; there were still two months before the dinner, and the entire membership selected the annual speaker because they considered this their big event of the year. So the program committee put together a list of several possible speakers, checking first to be sure the people could come on that date, and then they asked the entire membership to vote on the final choice. Mrs. Pimper was quite nice, and I told her I could indeed come at that time if finally invited. I also told her how flattered I was that the club wanted to include me even on the list of possible speakers.

I assumed Mrs. Pimper was white, not only because of her accent on the telephone (not always a certain clue) but also because I assumed the majority of business and professional women in Rome would be white, even if there were some black women in that select body. It never entered my mind that the club women in Rome also assumed that I was white.

A few days after the first contact Mrs. Pimper called again, full of enthusiasm, saying that the members had voted on their choice of speaker and wanted me to come. She asked that I send a photo and biography at once so that they could start the publicity. It should be a great evening, she said. But just a few days later this same woman who had seemed so friendly called again. "Xernona," she said, "are you sitting down?" I said, yes, not sure what she meant. "I am so mad," she said, "and if you want to sue, then I think you ought to sue."

Well, that was a pleasant way to begin a conversation.

"Guess what happened?" she asked. "You will never guess what happened." It seems that one lady on the program committee had seen the picture of me soon after it was sent to the club and exclaimed, "What! We have to have an emergency meeting. I had no idea she was black." They held their meeting, and five of the seven women on the committee professed to be astounded at discovering my skin hue. They insisted that Rome was not ready for a black woman to speak to their white women's group, that this was too big a step for them to take. Mind you, this was *1987*, not 1967. "I am so angry," I still remember Mrs. Pimper saying.

They decided to rescind the invitation, and they asked Mrs. Pimper to call me back and make excuses. "Tell her anything," they said. "Tell her we've changed the format or changed the date or changed the event; just tell her not to come."

Mrs. Pimper was fairly new to Rome, having moved there only three years before. She had truly enjoyed working with this women's club and believed it was a group she would continue to enjoy. But now she told the other women on the program committee that she wanted no part of their kind of hypocrisy, that she was resigning from the organization. "I am going to call Xernona, all right," she said, "but I am going to tell her the truth."

So you can see why I think Amy Pimper is the real heroine of this story. She called and told me the truth, and I think I can say with all honesty that initially I was not angry, perhaps because Amy was angry enough for both of us, and I admired her courage for speaking up in a difficult situation.

"Perhaps this is the way bigoted people operate," I told her, "but they still have a right to change their minds." I tried to muster a tone of dignity, telling Amy not to be upset and reminding her that they have the right to invite and they certainly have the right to disinvite. I told her that Dr. King had said so often that white people of good will would be the key to whatever progress black Americans would make in American society, that the struggle would continue until enough white people of good will united with us. "Amy," I told her, "you have demonstrated to me that you are one of the people who will help us achieve our rightful place in society, and I applaud you for it."

But by the next day I started to feel angry because I felt so rejected. I got more angry the more I thought about it. My attitude of restraint and dignity while talking to Amy did not represent my true feelings, I discovered.

Now, I had no intention of suing anybody, nor am I sure there was any ground for a lawsuit, except perhaps for the emotional distress I had suffered. Nor did I intend the occurrence to become a media event. I had good friends in the media who might have done a story if I had contacted them, but I did not. It was actually some days later that I happened to attend a dinner where I was sitting next to Tom Teepen, editorial page editor of the *Atlanta Constitution*, and he asked me what I had been up to recently. I wasn't doing a lot just then, I told him, other than feeling this great dose of rejection, and I told him how a group of white women had disinvited me to a big occasion in Rome. That was all the conversation we had about it, except for my general comment that I had been espousing the cause of women in my recent speeches, applauding women's achievements, noting that we as women were on the same path now, regardless of race or age or physical looks or whatever. I thought that most other women felt this also, a common sympathy beyond race, I said, but maybe I was mistaken because my Rome adventure had certainly left me feeling abused.

Teepen's column about my experiences ran in the next Saturday's paper, after he had called people in Rome to check out the story.

"Rednecks and primitives," he wrote, "took the fall for the racial hooliganism against brotherhood marchers in Forsyth County earlier this year. They did not represent, it was widely said, 'the good people.'

"Well, meet the good people of Rome, Georgia. Some of the good ones, anyway. They have just dis-invited a banquet speaker after finding out, to their surprise, that she is black. Rome, they said, is not ready to listen to a black speaker, and most particularly its Business and Professional Women's Club is not . . . ."

Teepen quoted me as saying that the incident had "knocked the reality back into me." I kept thinking that it really was *1987*, and yet something like this could still happen. I was a woman who had spoken out on women's issues, and these women in Rome were not ordinary women; these were the achievers, the intelligent women, the intellectual and educated women. These were the women doers, the decision makers, the elite of the community, the leaders. And they were saying, "No we won't have this; we can't have a black woman speaking at our annual dinner." Things were supposed to be getting better, I kept thinking to myself, but was this an example of it?

Teepen's column ran on Saturday, and the Rome newspaper, the *Rome News-Tribune*, picked up on it immediately. They ran that column in their Sunday paper and they also ran their own news story. Mrs. Pimper confirmed to the Rome newspaper that she had resigned from the club when they disinvited me to their banquet. "The very bad thing about this," she was quoted as saying, "is that Rome is going to get a black eye. I know it doesn't deserve it."

The other women on the program committee offered the newspaper a different version. Race had nothing to do with their decision to disinvite me to their dinner, they said. They had simply discovered what a famous person I was, what a celebrity, and they were afraid that the two-hundred-seat Krannert Center at Berry College, where their banquet was to be held, would simply not be big enough. It would be like, they said, asking the president of the United States to come to an elementary school. Their explanation was like, ridiculous.

"Something bad happens, something good can come out of it," my father used to say.

Some wonderful things began to happen.

I discovered when I read the news story in the Rome newspaper that there were *two* chapters of the Business and Professional Women's Club in that community, the Rome B&PW and the Cherokee B&PW. One member of Cherokee, Julie Hilburn, who had been state B&PW president three years before, said that their club did not "operate" in the same way as the Rome Club, that the Rome B&PW was "old South," while Cherokee represented younger working women. "Our policy is open membership," she said, adding that her club had had blacks in the club and black speakers. The action of the Rome B&PW was "not very businesslike . . . not very professional," she concluded. Other media followed up and it became a national story.

The Rome B&PW club sent me a letter apologizing for "any embarrassment or inconvenience you have experienced," but the letter did not re-extend the invitation to speak, nor did it make any mention of race or why I had been disinvited in the first place. The Rome newspaper, however, ran a letter from a young woman, Sue Anne Gresham, which read in part: "I am twenty-one and speak on behalf of myself and many other members of Rome's younger generation. For the most part, we are proud of our heritage in Rome. However, there are times when we wish we had been born and raised anywhere else besides Rome. . . . Racism seems to rise out of a disrespect for humanity. A community, such as Rome, cannot truly flourish until these attitudes change. . . . Perhaps Amy Pimper's move will spark more noble Romans to emerge and deal openly with discrimination."

That letter cheered me. Then the national president of B&PW clubs, Mary Ray Oaken, weighed in with a strong response. "I nearly died when I heard about this," said Ms. Oaken, who was attending a B&PW state convention in Illinois. "I have never been so hurt and upset. If it's necessary," she went on, "I will come down this week to Georgia and appear with Xernona any place she wants me to and make any sort of statement she wants me to make."

My ego did not require so much, that the national president make a personal trip to Atlanta. Nonetheless, Ms. Oaken dispatched the group's national executive director, Linda Dorian, to Atlanta to apologize and also to extend an invitation to me to speak at the B&PW national convention in Hawaii in July.

Think of it! Here I had been barred, or at least *disinvited*, from speaking to a group of perhaps two hundred women in a single B&PW chapter. Now I was going to speak to their national meeting with many many times that number of people, the elite of an organization with 140,000 members over the country.

I then got another surprising telephone call. Howard M. Smith, a white member of the Floyd County Commission, contacted me and expressed his regret at what had happened. He was a member of the Rome Kiwanis Club, he said, and he wondered if I would come and speak to their civic club. I accepted with pleasure. This was perhaps one week after the first news story ran, and the Rome newspaper followed up with a story about how Xernona Clayton was going to speak in Rome after all. Smith was quoted in the story as saying that the Kiwanis Club issued the invitation because of the "sleazy manner in which she was insulted," which he said was "not representative of this community." Besides, he added, "I thought it would be a pretty good program for the club."

I accepted the invitation to speak at the Kiwanis Club in May, about three weeks after the time when I would have spoken to the women's club. Floyd County Police Chief Jim Free offered to escort me personally to the Kiwanis meeting to be sure there was no problem of any kind. I did not expect any problems, but I did receive three threatening letters from Rome, anonymous letters, saying I had better not come to speak, that danger would be following me. As a result, Chief Free even offered to drive over to pick me up in Atlanta and drive me to Rome. The chief of security at Turner Broadcasting decided to ride over to Rome with me and my husband, along with another security guard. This was all very low key; we did not publicize that I had been threatened or had security protection, but Chief Free did drive over to pick us up and we all drove to Rome together.

The Kiwanis Club met at the Holiday Inn and the luncheon was packed, standing room only, with every news agency in the area there. They told me they had never had so much news coverage for any event they had.

I talked about race relations, about how racial prejudice is one of the most despicable expressions of inhumanity. I told them of my shock at being disinvited by the women's club because I was black. I told them how I had asked myself, is this really happening in 1987? Was this the end of my own personal road toward improved race relations? No, I said, this was merely a detour. Maybe my rejection by the women's business club could have a positive outcome by forcing others to confront the reality of racism. I quoted what Dr. King used to say about hatred and racism being a cancer, how we must uncover it and expose it and search relentlessly for a cure.

The heroine of this story is still Amy Pimper, the woman who had the courage to confront racism without hesitation. I sent her a basket of flowers and a note while this was all going on, and when a television crew went to interview her she pointed at the basket and said, "Here are some flowers from my new friend Xernona Clayton." I called her before the Kiwanis meeting and asked if she would like to attend.

She first said she would plan to come and then called back to say she had decided not to come because she had been part of the story, too, and she did not want her presence to upstage or distract from my presence in any way. I thought that was another display of the quality of her character, so I went by her office to visit with her after the Kiwanis meeting. I wanted to know if her investment business had suffered because of what she had done. Not really, she said. Some people had called to say they were going to take their business away from her, but they were balanced by others who praised her and promised to do business with her in the future. Amy Pimper considered herself my new friend, and I was delighted to count her as one.

Howard Smith, the Floyd county commissioner who invited me to the Kiwanis Club, and his wife Micky and my husband and I also became good personal friends. They were in Atlanta for a meeting not long after and invited us to join them for dinner. Another time I was invited to speak to a black church, the Metropolitan United Methodist Church, in Rome as their Women's Day speaker, and when he saw the event noted in the paper, he called to say the four of us should have dinner after the program was over. In fact, he came to the church to hear me speak, and I introduced him to the church, though of course he was already well known in the community. So it turned out that we made a lasting friendship, another good result of a bad incident. Later, when Andrew Young decided to run for governor in 1990, Commissioner Smith called to say he would like to have a fundraiser for Andy. I put them in touch, and they worked out such an event.

Other good things happened in the next couple of months after the Kiwanis meeting, while I was planning for the B&PW meeting in Hawaii. City and state chapters of the B&PW, including ones in Arkansas, California, Louisiana, Mississippi, Georgia, Wisconsin, and Massachusetts, called to tell me they had passed resolutions denouncing the action of the Rome chapter. The Tennessee state group called to say that I had a standing invitation to speak to them, that they would welcome a woman of my credentials any time.

The national B&PW convention in Hawaii was in mid-July, and I arrived on a Saturday. I was to speak on Sunday, as the keynote speaker for the first day of the conference. I had no idea what the size of the audience would be but simply appreciated the invitation, even if my audience turned out to be no more than the two hundred people who would have been at the Rome banquet. Indeed, some of the conference officials warned me that the attendance might not be great because a lot of people regarded Sunday as a kind of free day at the beginning of the conference and tended to go to the beach or take sightseeing tours.

I did not care; I was simply happy to be there. Some women attending recognized me in the hotel lobby and greeted me with such warm good wishes. There were three beautiful bouquets waiting in my room, absolutely gorgeous. "From your native home," read a card from the Georgia delegation; "we're glad you are here." Another was from the national office of the B&PW, and the third was signed, "Women who admire you." I never knew exactly who sent that one. My husband's cousin from Flint, Michigan, Adrienne Oliver, with whom I am very close, had traveled with me, and we both felt really good about the warm reception from everyone.

I don't often get nervous before crowds, but somehow I felt tension the next morning. I felt that a lot was expected of me. Did I deserve all this attention because of being disinvited by the Rome club? Also, I felt there might be some women there who would feel angry with me because of the media coverage of the controversy in Rome. These negative feelings consumed me on the morning of my speech, and I finally had to give myself a little talk and pull myself together. I had gotten a good night's rest, and I showered and took great pains dressing and applying my makeup, needing to feel that I looked my very best.

I did not know what to expect when I went downstairs to the ballroom, but having been warned that attendance could be low on the first day of the conference, I thought there might be two hundred to three hundred people. When I got to the ballroom, I actually thought I must be on the wrong floor, some other convention, because the crowd was so big that I could not believe at first that it was for me. The ballroom was set up for 4,800 people, I learned later, and so many people crowded in that there were probably more than five thousand in attendance. It was really overwhelming, initially.

The president, Mary Ray Oaken, introduced me to what became thunderous, resounding, standing applause.

My speech was entitled, "On the Road to Rome," and I began by saying, "Guess who is *not* coming to dinner in Rome?" It got us off to a laughing start, and I think they realized then that I was not some hostile woman who had come to chide all women in America because of the actions of one small group.

I also joked with them about what went through my mind when their executive director came to see me and invited me to speak in Hawaii, all expenses paid. I had shown great restraint, I said, because I had learned from my show business friends during my years in Los Angeles that you *must* play hard to get. So I had put on my best Hollywood act, first saying that I was not really sure I could accept the invitation, that I was so chagrined by what had happened in Rome that I would have to think about it. Little did the woman know, I said, that as soon as she was out of my office I ran home and started packing immediately, getting my leis and my muumuus out for the trip. They roared with laughter.

Turning serious, I told them that Dr. King would say that there is no hope, no future for any of us, if we continue to exclude people for something as superficial as race and color, that black Americans could only resolve such problems when they were joined by white people of *good will* who understood that injustice is injustice and that if it can happen to anybody it also can happen to you or me. I said I was still searching for such white people of good will.

The civil rights struggle at its height compelled Dr. King to remind us all that in the sight of God we were all the same, that hunger knows no color, pain knows no color, sadness and joy know no color. You could watch television and see people whose language you did not understand, but when they cried you could recognize their pain and when they laughed you could recognize their joy. We had to overcome our differences, I said, and understand the things we have in common. On my recent trip to Rome, there were stumbling blocks and detours but I ultimately got there and made some good friends there, and that road led onward to my being with this group in Hawaii.

The response of that group when I finished washed over me with a warmth which I will never forget. There was a standing ovation that seemed to go on forever. Someone told me later it lasted a good fifteen minutes; I don't know, but I felt such a lump in my throat that I really did not know what to do. I am not powerful enough as an orator or important enough to warrant such an ovation, but I got it. Then the president got up and presented me with a gift and said to the audience, "Do we love Xernona?" and the standing ovation started again for several more minutes. I still get goosebumps of excitement when I think about it; it was that overwhelming!

A lot of delegates asked to have their picture taken with me after the meeting broke up. I remember one woman from the Mississippi chapter who told me, "I'm from Mississippi and I know prejudice, I know segregation. I was taught it and I was reared on it, but somewhere along the way I went on that road to change, and today you made me feel guilty again for all those years before I did change." She thanked me for coming and wanted to have her photograph taken with me, and she said she would get her hometown newspaper to run it. I can't tell you how many invitations were extended to me to speak at state or local B&PW meetings, but I know I spent a lot of time over the next year or so traveling to make such speeches.

Reflecting later, after the meeting in Hawaii, I thought again of what my father told me so often, that the things that are perhaps your biggest deterrents are things over which you exert little control. I did not choose to be black, nor did others choose to be white; none of us have choice in certain basic givens. We did not choose our parents, nor our color, nor our sex. We are denied that opportunity to choose; we don't have that divine authority, yet all our basic human beginnings are identical. We go astray after we enter a society which may teach us to adopt prejudicial views. It is so stifling to our psychological growth to be prejudiced in our thinking because *that* changes our behavior. Unfortunately, our behavior often speaks louder than our words.

Oh Daddy, you are still right!

And right also that when something bad happens, something good can come from it.

Twenty

I met my present husband, Paul Brady, after he came to Atlanta in the early 1970s as a federal administrative law judge. Now, I was not looking for a husband. I had been a widow for the better part of a decade, and I had an exceedingly full and active life. I was hosting my own television show, active in the community, and I enjoyed the company of a lot of good friends. I am simply not one of these women who have just *got* to find a husband if temporarily without one, and I was not interested in blind dates. I was self-sufficient and independent, and I was really not at all sure that I would ever remarry.

Then along came Paul.

He had been married as a young man and then divorced, and his two children, Laura and Paul, Jr., were thirteen and fourteen years old at the time. Paul, too, had a full life, a highly successful career as a practicing attorney with energy enough to be active in all kinds of other projects. He became the first black attorney with the Federal Power Commission and then was named a federal judge in 1972. I am not sure Paul had any notion that he would ever remarry either. Had it not been for our mutual friend Betty Griffin, we probably never would have gotten together. She pressured us to meet, and we did so reluctantly, but we came to love each other and decided indeed that we wanted to spend the rest of our lives together.

We had a June wedding in 1974 and the *Atlanta Daily World* ran a photograph of my cutting the wedding cake, with Paul standing at my side. The caption below the picture called it "Wedding of the Year." Some eight hundred of our friends and family were there. Earlier, the *New York Times Magazine* ran a story with a full-color photograph on the front cover from our engagement party at the home of Lillian and now-Congressman John Lewis.

Paul has this terrible habit of teasing me by saying to people that he had married an "older woman," which of course is not true, and besides all our friends would tell you how much younger I look than he does. Anyway, I decided to get even as his sixtieth birthday approached in 1987 by having a birthday party for him and letting all his friends know how old he *really* was. He is truly very supportive of the many things I do and always manages to maintain his good humor in escorting me to the many formal dinners I attend in the course of duty. So on the night of his birthday he thought he was taking me to one more black-tie banquet at the Omni Hotel in Atlanta. I had assembled his brothers and sisters, batches of nieces and nephews, and carloads of cousins from over the country for a family weekend, and Paul knew nothing about their presence or about the surprise birthday party.

There was a crowd of four hundred people there and they greeted him with cries of "Here comes the Judge." The honoree was a bit flabbergasted as he then received tributes from Coretta Scott King, Bob Wussler of Turner Broadcasting, City Councilman Hosea Williams, the Rev. Ralph Abernathy, Atlanta Mayor Andrew Young, Congressman John Lewis, Judges H. T. Lockhard, James D. Burroughs, Thelma Wyatt Cummings, William Fowler, Horace Ward, and Clarence Cooper, and Georgia Secretary of State Max Cleland. One of the judges there, Louis Simmons of Detroit, judge on the

Third Circuit Court of Wayne County, grew up with my husband. They shined shoes together in segregated hotels, and now in another era both administer justice proudly, with an eye to overcoming discrimination and being equally fair to all groups of people.

I remember teasing Paul, "You better enjoy yourself, because the best part of all this is that all of these people are your guests, so you get to pay the whole bill."

When Paul and I decided to get married, I took each of his children, Laura and Paul, to lunch to talk to them individually about my future role in their lives. The children were extremely close to their father and cherished the relationship they had shared over a long period of time. When Paul lived at home, he was an attentive father, and the close relationship he had established continued after he and his wife divorced. At that time, they were living in Michigan with their mother, Dr. Betty Brady, a university professor, and they spent all of their vacation time with their father. The children, whom I had met but not come to know, were beautiful and seemed well mannered, well disciplined, and happy. Our discussions at lunch went very well, and I thought everything was in order to have a successful union. I think I expected us to become one big happy family overnight. It didn't happen quite that way.

Laura was a sweeet, demurring young lady, very cooperative and obliging and wanted everything to go smoothly. As a matter of fact, she said I "freed" her from the chauvinistic inclinations of the male-dominated trio. When the three of them were together, Daddy Paul and Brother Paul would relegate "female" jobs to her ... dishes, sweeping, dusting, washing, etc. When I arrived on the scene, I eliminated all of that. We became a "liberated" family. She seemed very happy with the additional support I gave her, and she adapted very easily to the changes. The adjustment period was a little more difficult for our son, Paul. He saw my presence as a real threat to the tranquility and easy movement of the three of them. Sharing his father's attention was not at all easy for him, and the disruption was a little more traumatic.

We all looked to make the transition a harmonious one. Each of us had to compromise, and with love, persistence, understanding, and patience, we all won. We eventually became the one big happy family we all wanted. The real testament to our victory came when Laura said that she and her brother were more blessed than most children. They had three wonderful parents who loved, nurtured, and disciplined them. Whether they were in Michigan with their mother or in Atlanta with us, there was constant communication. They were never without warmth, guidance, and caring.

One of the keys to our success was that each of us parents realized how important it was to acknowledge and accept the fact that the others had an important role in the child's life. My husband understood the need for me to establish and implement rules of discipline in our household, and he learned to respect that. Betty, whom I describe and identify endearingly as my "wife-in-law," accepted my style of discipline, and we respected her rules in her house, but I always tried to remain neutral when issues arose between my husband and Betty. We all had one mission in mind—love, protect, guide, nurture, and teach the children and pray they would end up as sound, responsible, decent, productive, and happy adults.

Our mission was accomplished. We are three proud parents with two wonderful children. Dr. Laura Brady is a registered pharmacist in Atlanta, and Sgt. Paul Brady proudly serves his country in the United States Marine Corps.

•   •   •

Quite coincidentally, Paul and I are both having autobiographical books published within the same few months. His book is a remarkable one, much of it about Paul's family and his own personal experiences, but much of it also historical, carefully researched, about the patterns of racial discrimination in our country since the earliest days.

The title of his book, *A Certain Blindness*, comes from a lecture given by the famous Harvard psychologist William James in 1892, referring to the blindness individuals often display towards the feelings and values of others. It is Paul's view that the white majority of Americans has often "willfully blinded itself to the humanity and worth of Americans of African descent in order to preserve the best portion for itself." Paul recognized that there was a glaring lack of understanding between white and black Americans due largely to a biased and distorted view of our history and of the injustices suffered by African-Americans. This distorted perspective has caused "a certain blindness" to current racial problems.

Paul writes about how thousands and tens of thousands of black Americans have fought for their country since the early days of our nation, yet rarely have their achievements been recorded in the standard history books. Crispus Attucks, a black man who led a group of patriotic citizens against a British garrison in Boston, was the first American to die in the American Revolution and for that reason his name is relatively well known. Yet how many Americans, even black Americans, know that President Andrew Jackson, while he was General Jackson, recruited black troops to help defend New Orleans in the War of 1812? Or that those black troopers performed magnificently, not only holding their portion of the line against trained British soldiers but then launching a successful counterattack? General Jackson issued a proclamation after the battle, declaring that he had expected much of these black troops when he asked them to serve, but adding, "You have done more than I expected . . . Soldiers! The president of the United States shall hear how praiseworthy was your conduct in the hour of danger; and the representatives of the American people will give you the praise your exploits entitle you to."

But that did not happen. Slavery became more entrenched than ever after the War of 1812. The role of those black soldiers was forgotten. Those black veterans were in fact not even permitted to march in the annual parades celebrating that victory. Often, Paul notes, the hundreds of thousands of black Americans who have served in every war since then did so in the hope that their willingness to risk their lives for their country would help persuade their nation to grant them greater freedoms. Typically, they have been disappointed and their sometimes heroic deeds put out of mind.

Paul writes of another context in which the roles played by black Americans have been forgotten. As he was being sworn in as a federal judge in 1972, he recalls, his thoughts drifted to his great-uncle Bass Reeves, who was sworn in as a federal deputy marshal in Fort Smith, Arkansas in 1875, almost exactly a century earlier. The frontier lawmen of the American West were legendary, says Paul, with no stage better dramatizing the American spirit. The names of many such heroes are well known, like the Texas Rangers and Wild Bill Hickok and Bat Masterson. Few would know the name of Bass Reeves, he goes on, since our "history has not tended to report the stories of our black heroes."

Reeves worked as a deputy marshal for thirty-two years, serving Judge Isaac C. Parker, known as "Hanging Judge" Parker, for twenty-one of those years while Parker administered the law in the federal territory that later became the state of Oklahoma. Bass Reeves was born in slavery, on a cotton plantation in Texas. He was a favorite of his master in one way because he learned to shoot at an early age and was an incredible marksman with either rifle or pistol. His master encouraged this particular talent, letting Reeves sometimes demonstrate his skill for the amusement of the master's friends, but his owner refused when Reeves asked to be taught to read so that he could read the Bible for himself.

Reeves fled Texas and slavery and lived as a fugitive in the Oklahoma territory until after the Civil War. Then, as a free man, he practiced the peaceful profession of farming, until President Ulysses S. Grant named Judge Isaac C. Parker federal judge for the Western District of Arkansas (as the Oklahoma territory was then called). Someone wrote later that Judge Parker's charge was to apply the law to the "worst band of desperadoes, murderers, and outlaws to be found in any civilized land." One of the judge's first actions was to seek out and swear in fearless men as chief marshal and deputy marshals to enforce the law, to bring these desperadoes in dead or alive. Paul's great-uncle was one of the first such marshals who, as the phrase went, "rode for Parker."

Reeves brought almost unique qualifications to the task, being a crack shot and knowing the territory, as he put it, "like a cook knows her kitchen." He had befriended many Indians while hiding out in that territory and he was fluent in Seminole, Creek, and Cherokee, and even in some lesser known Indian tongues. D. C. Gideon, whose book *Indian Territory* was published in 1901, wrote that no marshal in that time had "effected more hazardous arrests than Bass Reeves. . . . He fears nothing that moves or breathes. . . ."

There was a particular outlaw who drew Bass Reeves' special attention, one Bob Dozier, who had eluded the law for a number of crimes, and Reeves vowed to bring him in.

Dozier was not a very nice man. He had been a successful farmer for many years and then decided that outlaw life was more appealing. He had a lot of interests. He stole cattle, robbed stores and banks, and held up stagecoaches and cattle buyers carrying large amounts of money. He ambushed travelers, held up card players in big-money poker games, ran land swindles, and was the head of a horse rustling operation. Along the way, he murdered several people, and it was rumored that he had even tortured people in order to get information for some of his criminal enterprises.

Reeves began gathering information on Dozier, including a careful description because he had never seen him face to face, and for months he trailed him, sometimes coming close enough to send Dozier on the run. When Dozier found out who was chasing after him, he sent word that Reeves better leave him alone or he was a dead man. Reeves sent word if Dozier wanted to shoot him, at least he would have to stop running long enough to try it, and the marshal would be ready for that.

At one point, Reeves and another lawman were hot on Dozier's trail, believing that they were no more than an hour behind. But it started to rain, and they decided to give up for the night and dismounted to look for a dry place to sleep.

Reeves heard a shot, and a bullet passed by him all too near. It was an ambush and he and his companion dove for cover. The rain made it hard to see, but Reeves could make out the shadow of a man moving between two trees. He fired and saw the shadow fall. His shot revealed his own exact position and several other shots came whistling by him. Reeves stood up, moved out from the protection of the tree, and fell facing the shots that had just come his way, stretched out as if dead but with his pistol in his hand, cocked and ready. There was laughter as another man walked out from the trees, apparently assuming that Reeves *was* dead and that his companion had fled. Lightning flashed as the man neared, and Reeves saw that indeed it was Dozier. He rose up and demanded that Dozier surrender, and when Dozier tried to fire at him again, he shot him in the neck and killed him.

The hardest warrant Marshal Bass Reeves probably ever served came after he had just finished trailing three outlaws into the Indian territory. They had ambushed him and he had killed one of the three, then persuaded the other two that it was in their best interest to surrender. He brought them back to the federal jail in Muskogee, thinking that he had earned a little rest.

But, no, the chief marshal said to him that there was one more warrant he wanted him to serve. He hated to ask this of Bass, the chief marshal said, but he did not want to ask anyone else either. It was a warrant for the arrest of Marshal

Reeves' son, on a charge of murdering his wife, and the son was a fugitive somewhere in the Indian territory. It is hard to imagine what thoughts must have gone through the marshal's head, but he took the warrant and told the chief marshal that he was right, that Bass would not want anyone else to serve it, either. Two weeks later he returned with his son as prisoner, who was immediately bound over for trial. The local newspaper, the *Muskogee Daily Phoenix*, wrote about the incident, saying that Bass Reeves had "a devotion to duty equal to that of the old Roman Brutus, whose greatest claim to fame was that the love of his son could not sway him from justice."

The Indian territory became the state of Oklahoma in 1907 and other law enforcement agencies took over the roles of the marshals. Bass had served as federal marshal for thirty-two years and could have retired, but he chose to continue working with the Muskogee police force for two more years. His health began to fail rapidly in 1909, and he died in 1910 after a short illness.

Reeves' funeral was attended by hundreds of people, blacks and whites and Indians. The *Muskogee Daily Phoenix* ran a glowing obituary, saying that in "the history of the early days of Oklahoma the name of Bass Reeves has a place in the front rank among those who cleaned out the old Indian Territory of outlaws and desperadoes. No story of the conflict of the government's officers with those outlaws which ended only a few years ago with the rapid filling up of the territory with people, can be complete without mention of the old Negro who died yesterday. . . . He was sent to arrest some of the most desperate characters that ever infested Indian Territory and endangered life and peace in its borders . . . but Bass Reeves always said that he had never shot a man when it was not necessary for him to do so in the discharge of his duty or to save his own life."

The story fascinates me in part because this remarkable man was Paul's great-uncle. But remember also that I was born in Muskogee, Oklahoma and that decades later I grew up in the very same town where Marshal Bass Reeves used to ride his big sorrel horse when bringing his outlaw prisoners into the federal jail for transport to Fort Smith. Still more years later I would meet and marry the marshal's great-nephew in Atlanta, Georgia. People's families cross paths in strange and mysterious ways.

Is it any wonder that my husband Paul is proud of his great-uncle Bass Reeves?

Or that Paul thought of him while being sworn in as a federal judge?

Is it not easy to see why Paul believes that the name of Bass Reeves, had he been white, might be as well known today as the name of Wild Bill Hickock, Wyatt Earp, or Bat Masterson?

And is it not likely that, had he been white, we all would have seen one or more Western movies about this heroic lawman's life?

Another interesting bit of Paul's history was that he was on the scene for what became probably the most significant civil rights ruling ever handed down by the U.S. Supreme Court— *Brown v. Board of Education*, ordering the desegregation of public schools and declaring the old "separate but equal" doctrine unconstitutional.

Paul completed his military service in the U.S. Navy and returned home to Flint, Michigan, in 1947. He tried first to train for a career in auto engineering by enrolling in the General Motors Technical Institute. He was turned down because he was black. Then a former shipmate, Leroy Day, and he both got jobs in a railroad diesel plant, expecting to be trained in diesel engines since both had some experience with such engines in the Navy. That did not last long. They were soon told that they could not continue in the engine service department because there were more senior white workers who might want the jobs.

Paul was discouraged. But he decided that while still working with the railroad he would take advantage of a reduced fare available to employees and take a train to California to see the sights, stopping off to visit with his uncle and aunt, Alvin and Lucinda "Cindy" Todd in Topeka, Kansas.

His interests at that point in his life were divided between studying psychology and going to law school. His aunt and uncle urged him to think about coming to live in Topeka because the famous Menninger Foundation of psychiatric disciplines was there, as was Washburn University with its fine law school. He moved to Topeka and ended up completing law school at Washburn. Meanwhile, he became actively involved with that landmark case of *Brown v. The Board of Education of Topeka, Kansas* because his aunt happened to be one of the plaintiffs. She had been active with the NAACP as its secretary and in protesting segregation in the Topeka public schools as a way of seeking better opportunities for her daughter Nancy Todd (Paul's first cousin), now married to Ramon Noches.

Thurgood Marshall, special counsel for the NAACP, had once stayed as a guest in the home of Paul's uncle and aunt during the time when most hotels were totally segregated, and he was familiar with the school situation in Topeka. Paul's aunt agreed to join with twelve other plaintiffs in the lawsuit seeking relief from the segregated practices of their local public schools, and that historic case became what Louis H. P. Pollack, dean of Yale Law School, later called "the most important governmental act of any kind since the Emancipation Proclamation."

So Paul had the rare opportunity to be involved in such history while still a student. You can see why I am proud of him, even though it does concern me sometimes that I married a *much* older man.

Twenty-one

Once, when I was still young
and single and living in Chicago, a married man whom I
knew slightly called me and wanted to come to my home to
talk to me about something in great confidence. I was wary. I
had already run into some married men who wanted to visit
with me in confidence, and I knew what they had in mind.

I tried to say no, but he was very insistent that it was about
something important and that he must see me privately. I
finally agreed, not because I was intimidated but because I
suppose I have always had the idea that I could take care of
myself if need be and I certainly had no intention of getting
involved with a married man in any improper way.

This man was about forty, maybe just under six feet and of
strong build; he was enormously rich and lived in a large
beautiful mansion. It was believed that he ran a substantial
portion of the numbers racket in Chicago, but this was never
actually substantiated to my knowledge. I have thought since
that he was something like Scott Fitzgerald's Gatsby because
he had the beautiful big house and a lot of money from
possibly shady sources, yet he also wanted to be liked, to be
socially acceptable. He was dark-skinned and his wife was
fair-skinned. That was significant at that time because light

skin was more esteemed in the black community, or so it appeared. He was clearly proud of his wife and urged her to take part in the social functions of the community, especially in all the charitable causes, to which they donated generously. The source of his income was never discussed.

I knew the man slightly because his wife and I had gotten involved in some of the same volunteer charity organizations. She looked good and dressed well, and their three children went to good private schools. Getting involved in the right kind of charities was a good way for her to appear in legitimate community settings and she certainly did that. We worked together on one big charitable fundraising project, and she began to invite us to her home for the committee meetings on a regular basis. It was quite nice of her; she was offering us the comfort of her home and would serve us refreshments, and the work went well in that atmosphere.

She was a well-organized woman, quick to understand the details of our fundraising, and she would sometimes even offer to donate her own funds to match those raised in all the rest of the community. So her presence on the committee virtually guaranteed a successful campaign. I got to know her husband at least by name because he would sometimes come in or go out while we were meeting at their home. It was slight acquaintance, but I knew who he was and he knew who I was.

I was absolutely amazed, however, when he asked to come over that day. I was also suspicious, hesitant, and reluctant, but I did not want him to think that I was fearful, and I *did* have this notion that I could take care of myself. Also, something in the tone of his plea began to make me listen to him in a different way. It was highly confidential, he kept saying; he could not meet me anywhere in public, and he hoped I would honor his request that we meet in private.

I gave it some thought and finally, with trepidation, agreed to let him visit me at my home. Yet I still half believed that he was coming to try to get familiar, and I worried about the fact that I really liked his wife and didn't want to get involved in even the appearance of a triangle. Being a single woman in Chicago had not always been easy, but I had certainly managed successfully to stay clear of those kinds of involvements. At any rate, I had all these wild ideas about what he might say or do, that he might offer me money to lure my attention or I don't know what.

To my great relief, he made no personal advances at all but he repeated what he had said on the telephone, that he had something very serious to discuss with me in confidence. He seemed so serious that his manner put me at ease, and I forgot all those suspicions I had entertained previously. It seemed more like a business meeting really, until he shocked me with his request. First, however, he proceeded with a litany of his accomplishments.

He was an impressive man in appearance, confident in manner and well dressed. I remember that evening he was wearing a camel-colored vicuna coat. He told me how successful he had been in his business operation, how much property he had acquired, how many automobiles he had. He went through a list of such attainments, all evidence of his success. Then he told me his big confidential secret.

He had never learned to read.

He absolutely could not read at all. He could recognize his own name in writing and he could handle numbers, but that was all. He could not even read his children's names, not in the sense of understanding what the letters signified, but he had carefully learned how to recognize the names of each of his three kids by taking a fatherly interest when each became old enough to write his or her name.

That was a large part of his concern. Now that his children were getting older he was afraid they would realize that their father could not read—or write, for that matter. He could recognize some few other names, names of people important to him, but that was it. I asked him how he could run a business with such a limitation, and he told me that since he could understand numbers and figures, he could review what his bookkeeper reported to him. Even the bookkeeper did not know that he could not read because he could sign his name, so he and the bookkeeper would talk about expenditures and then he would just sign the checks. It was really that his children were getting older that made him worry about it, because he didn't want them to know.

So what he wanted from me was nothing personal or intimate at all. He wanted *me* to teach *him* how to read. I asked him why he chose me to be his tutor, because although I was a schoolteacher I had never done any private tutoring at all. He picked me, he said, because everyone who knew me spoke highly of my good character and integrity, and he knew I was active in church. He felt that I was honest, a person he could trust with a confidential matter. That was what worried him so, what really consumed him, that he desperately wanted to learn to read but he just as desperately did not want anyone to find out what he was doing. He said he had observed me at his home at the volunteer committee meetings with his wife, and he had finally decided that I was a person he could trust with this secret.

He offered to pay me for my tutoring, but that was not really a factor. I was just so touched that he wanted to learn and to spare his children that embarrassment that I happily agreed to teach him.

I was not at all a professional tutor, so I simply used my own common sense. I went to the educational resource store and got basic reading materials, and we set up regular tutoring sessions. I worried that anyone seeing him coming to my house might get the wrong idea, the same idea that had entered my head when he first called, and I said to him that his meeting with me so privately worried me because his wife could learn of the meetings and misinterpret them. His wife was not the kind of person to check up on him, he said, but he agreed that if she ever became suspicious he would tell her about the lessons. He would not want to harm my reputation.

He insisted that his wife had no idea he couldn't read, and I suppose that is possible. But I knew her as a rather smart woman, and it was my guess that she was aware of his lack of education but shrewdly chose never to mention it.

Our tutoring sessions went on for about six months, perhaps a little longer. He was an accomplished man and he was smart, so he caught on pretty rapidly. We started using newspapers and magazines and flip cards with the ABCs, while I showed him how you put letters together to make words. He wasn't planning to write a graduate school thesis, so I concentrated on short words and sentences. He already spoke well, so I would show him sentences in a newspaper or magazine that were similar to something he might say in conversation. I was groping along as a tutor, but my methods seemed to work well.

I ended up thinking of this tutoring as a great challenge and didn't intend to charge him anything, but he insisted on giving me a nice monetary reward when we completed the task. I think of this really as another example of how you can make a change in another person's life just by doing what you can. It ties in with my whole general philosophy, that whenever you can help somebody *go ahead and do it*. That tutoring did not take anything much from me, in time or anything else, but it changed that man's life and gave me the greatest possible satisfaction.

•　　•　　•

Connecting with people, or, sometimes, helping other people connect has always been the most rewarding kind of experience for me.

I remember that when Stokely Carmichael became head of the Student Non-Violent Coordinating Committee in the mid-1960s, his rhetoric startled black people and white people alike. It pained Dr. King so much because of his own personal commitment to the principle of non-violence. During that time he would often meet with the SNCC students and talk about mutual strategies and how to coordinate their energies to focus on issues of concern. Stokely caused Dr. King great agony one night by coming out with his famous slogan, "black power." It may have been only rhetoric for some, but the news stories about it got national and international attention, and many read it as a denunciation of all white people. Dr. King did not believe in that, of course, and the SCLC and SNCC went in different directions after that time. Dr. King never contemplated separating people or hating white people. He felt that all people of good will should work together to bring about positive change.

So Stokely's rhetoric frightened a lot of people. Yet I knew him and I continued to help him, though certainly not with anything violent or anti-anybody. I had always been the kind of citizen who had good friends and resources, and I could sometimes raise money by contacting people who were committed to civil rights or other humanitarian causes. I had helped Stokely in that way, so it was not a great surprise when he called me at home one night. The SNCC group was really in a bind, he told me, because they were supposed to get some students over to a town in Alabama for a demonstration and they simply had no money at all. They needed to raise $500 for transportation, he said, and they were calling their friends for help. They really needed the $500, he said, but they could probably squeeze by on $300.

As it happened, I was having a dinner party that evening that included some white friends who were quite well informed about the civil rights movement, including the "black power" direction SNCC had recently taken. But I explained to Stokely that my friends were people of good will and if he would come over to my house I would try to prevail on them to contribute some money.

Then, when I got off the telephone, I told my friends that Stokely Carmichael was on his way over to ask them for money. A couple of my friends looked at me in amazement and said, "Stokely Carmichael? You mean the guy who hates white people?" "Right," I told them, "this is the guy who hates white people." But then I gave them my spiel. I would not ask them to give money to fund Stokely's radical "black power" posturing, I said, but this was a case of SNCC trying to get some students over to a particular community where there had been racial tensions, where they were needed to protest specific injustices, and I thought that their mission was one we could all support.

My friends were agreeable and they let me take up the collection. I made a different spiel to Stokely when he got to my house. I told him I wanted him to count the money on the spot — it was roughly $350 — and I told him this was how we brought about change, not by hating white people but by asking them to support those causes that make for justice. I told him I could not have afforded to give him three hundred dollars, let alone five hundred, but the white friends in my home had raised that money so he and the other students could seek justice and change.

Stokely took the money and thanked each of my white guests for helping. He was a charming and good-looking young man, and my guests saw for themselves that he could be a nice person. Stokely was smart and shrewd, and looking back I think maybe his "black power" scare tactics were intended for deliberate effect. The rhetoric frightened some white people, who then saw Dr. King and others in a better and more moderate light. But that night at my house was one for togetherness, and it was a good experience for all of us.

•　　•　　•

I have often thought of how much impact both the King family and the Kennedy family have had on my own life and on the lives of so many others and how those two families fought for the same just causes and how each family was touched by such great tragedy. It was President John Kennedy's call for volunteers that got me involved with the school dropout program in California.

One particularly sad experience comes to mind. The night Senator Robert Kennedy was killed in Los Angeles, my close personal friend Ross Miller was with the senator and his entourage. Dr. Miller, a noted surgeon, was pressed into duty to lend medical assistance to the fallen senator and accompanied him to the emergency room of the Los Angeles hospital.

It was Dr. Miller who was interviewed by the national media regarding the condition of the senator, and I watched the television with a mixture of pride and pain. The pride came from the fact that my good friend was responding to the interviewers' questions so professionally and proficiently despite the traumatic encounter he had witnessed first-hand. The pain came with the anguish I felt from the tragic loss of a great human spirit; it was a pain, obviously, that the whole nation was feeling.

I also remember when the SCLC invited Senator Edward Kennedy to speak at its annual meeting in 1966 in Jackson, Mississippi, the first such meeting after Dr. King asked me to take over the planning and arrangements. There was a threat against Senator Kennedy just before his arrival, a threat that turned out to have some substance to it.

I had gone to the police chief of Jackson when I first visited to check the hotel arrangements and other details. He was courteous and friendly and said that times were changing fast, even in Jackson, and he did not anticipate any racial tensions or trouble. He did add, though, that this SCLC group was the first convention of blacks ever to gather at a previously all-white downtown hotel. The hotel people were nice, too, and I assured them that we were not going to burn the building down, even if most of our delegates were black.

Now, I had arranged for a car to pick up special VIP guests at the airport, but on the day Senator Kennedy was arriving I heard on the radio a rumor that somebody was going to stop him as he got off the plane, not let him reach downtown Jackson to speak to the SCLC convention. This was only a rumor, according to the broadcast, but such reports are so hard to assess. Was this some kind of scare tactic, or was it a real threat? I called the chief of police, who assured me that nothing bad was going to happen, but at my urging he agreed to send two unmarked police cars out to the airport to provide security for the senator. I actually had two cars at my disposal, a limousine appropriate for Senator Kennedy to ride in and an older, more ordinary car. I decided to ask the senator to ride in the less conspicuous car. This proved not a bad idea.

Our small motorcade had one police car in front, then the limousine, then the more ordinary car, and then the second police car. The first car suddenly had a blowout and then the limousine swerved, too. Someone had spread hundreds of long tacks on the road, heavy enough to cause blowouts, and those first two cars both ended up in a small ditch. The police quickly cleared the tacks from the road, and the other police car and the small car with Senator Kennedy in it sped rapidly into downtown. Maybe it was just harassment, but it is hard to know. If we had been without the police and the car with Senator Kennedy in it had been stopped, maybe someone would have really tried to do him harm.

The police chief came to see me at the hotel that evening and commented that sometimes you underestimated potential dangers and that maybe the combination of King and Kennedy and black people staying at the downtown hotel for the first time was enough to create some kind of trouble. The police chief was very guarded in his conversation with me, but I felt that he believed that someone had really set out to hurt Senator Kennedy. There were no other incidents, though. The senator made his speech to the SCLC meeting that evening, and it pleased me that he praised me to Dr. King for arranging the security at the airport.

Senator Kennedy, Dr. King and Coretta, and I and several others just sat around in one of the hotel suites, laughing and joking, until it was time for him to leave for his plane. It was the first time most of us in the suite that night had had that kind of intimate and friendly contact with a Kennedy. The Kennedy and King families have touched and influenced my life in myriad ways. Truly, few American families have had so much impact on the hearts and minds of so many.

Twenty-two

My religious faith has been strong throughout my life. I know for certain that I am a blessed individual, blessed by the good Lord, though I am not one to stand on street corners and shout it to everybody. My faith is part of my past and my present and, I hope, my future. I hope I will have lived the kind of life that might meet the requirements to go to a better place, the place we call Heaven. I hold to my faith and I try to live it. It is the mainstay of my life.

So many things have happened to me. I believe I had some preparation to meet the challenges I have faced, but I also think a great portion of what has happened to me has been a blessing from the good Lord. I know I am especially blessed in having had good health for my whole life up until now. And I think I am of sound mind, of some mental agility and strength. My constant prayer has been that God will give me the strength to face and stand up under the pressures of the day, to meet the obstacles that people place in my path, and I believe that God has answered that prayer. I do meet obstacles, some meant for me, some accidental, and the Lord has helped me cope with those challenges.

I have also been blessed in that every era of my life has

been so interesting. Chicago was a fast town, an exciting town, when my sister and I first moved there in the 1950s. It seemed that there were men standing on every corner waiting for girls to get off the buses or trains, offering to show them the ropes, *their* version of the ropes. But my sister and I did pretty well in Chicago governing our own lives, directing our own paths, doing what we wanted to do and meeting a lot of wonderful people. We picked our own dates; we didn't fall for cheap come-ons but chose men with whom we developed mutual admiration. Chicago was a wide open town then, and we knew girls who got caught up in dire situations because a man offered them something that sounded attractive—free rent, say, or a holiday in New York. Somehow, my sister and I came to Chicago prepared to deal with the enticements of the big city, the seductions of a fast lifestyle. We felt self-sufficient and paid our own rent and governed our own lives. And it was a fun period, an exciting time, and Chicago was an exciting city. I just absolutely loved living in Chicago.

My California time was exciting in a different way. Los Angeles was the entertainment capital of the world, and the black entertainers all wanted to be in *Jet* magazine, so my husband Ed and I got invitations to all kinds of parties, openings, and celebrations. We also became friends with a lot of people who were not connected to *Jet*. David Brown at Twentieth Century Fox and his administrative assistant Pamela Hedley became good personal friends and remain friends to this day. Because of them I had free access to the studios, and before long I was on a first-name basis with actor Dick Powell and his wife June Allyson. Ed and I always got invited to the Academy Awards and had the chance to meet movie stars like Elizabeth Taylor and Charlton Heston, people I had read about and admired for years.

Atlanta is my city now, and I have felt its growth since I first moved here in the 1960s, a time then when there was not an expressway from downtown to the Atlanta airport. Now there are not only expressways but a modern rapid transit system and a spectacular new international airport. There are hotels and restaurants that compare well with any in the world and wonderful universities and churches, not to mention CNN, which demonstrated during the Persian Gulf war that it is probably the best news organization in the world. Finally, there are a great many fine people who strive to build what Congressman John Lewis calls the "beloved community."

. . .

My fondest memories include wonderful teachers who helped mold my understanding of life and who worked daily to give us the strong moral guidance and the "seriousness" of education. Two of my elementary school chums remain my friends today, and I am in regular contact with Marverine Givens and Celestine Johnson, both still living in Muskogee, Oklahoma. I value those long-term relationships, as well as the friendships I formed in college.

One of the highest honors I could receive came from the American Intercultural Student Exchange when they named a scholarship in my honor. The Xernona Clayton Scholarship affords a minority student the opportunity to live abroad for a year with all expenses paid. It has been my delight to select such a student each year since 1987, five so far.

How can one describe the feeling of joy when Hadassah, the Jewish women's organization, plants a tree in your honor in Freedom Forest in Israel? I had the awesome pleasure of visiting Freedom Forest when I was invited to Israel and spent ten exciting days as guest of the Israeli government. One of the highlights of that trip in 1973 was an exclusive television interview with Prime Minister Golda Meir. I took my sister along with me and we took side trips to Italy and enjoyed the ruins and religious sites of Rome.

The benevolence of John H. Johnson, publisher of *Jet* and *Ebony* magazines, goes beyond description. A few years into my first marriage, my husband suffered a heart attack, subsequently contracted tuberculosis from a co-worker, was hospitalized for three months and was incapacitated for a total of six months. Long after the normally alloted sick leave, Mr. Johnson continued to send Ed's paycheck for an uninterrupted period of convalescense and called me almost daily to ask what I needed.

I feel a heightened pride when, each Christmas, children from disadvantaged neighborhoods are invited to an Annual Christmas Party hosted by the Southern Christian Leadership Conference. I proposed the idea to host such an event to Dr. King in 1966; we entertained one hundred children the first year, and now that project has expanded to thousands. There's a saying that "there's no such thing as a small idea" (or something to that effect), and there is an inner feeling of joy when your idea ends up producing great results for an important group of people — in this case, children who otherwise might not have such a merry Christmas!

•   •   •

We have come a long way since the early 1960s when almost everything was still racially segregated — most public schools and other public facilities, hotels and restaurants, even swimming pools and water fountains. But there are still prejudices enough, social and economic barriers erected on the basis of race or sex. The good fortune and successful career that I have enjoyed are a testimony to social progress, yet it was only four years ago that I was "disinvited" to speak to Rome's Business and Professional Women's Club.

As I look back now, it pleases me to note how many changes there have been, how many battles, large and small, have been waged and won against racial discrimination. But I also ponder how far we still have to go.

I remember many little things, though perhaps they were not so little after all. In Los Angeles, for example, the streets were cleaned on a definite schedule, usually two times each week. The street cleaners might clean one side of a street one day and the other side the next day, and they would put up a sign telling you which side to park your car on. After I had been in Atlanta for about a week, it dawned on me that I had not seen any signs about when the street cleaners came. I asked the people at the SCLC what kind of schedule the sweepers kept near their offices since I didn't want to park my car on the wrong side of the street, and they looked at me blankly. They didn't know what in the world I was talking about.

What I discovered was that the streets in the black community, like Auburn Avenue, were rarely cleaned and certainly not on any regular schedule. I immediately called City Hall, got connected to the right department, and said I wanted to know when the street by our offices would be cleaned. First I was told that nobody knew the exact schedule, and then I was told that the city's equipment had broken down. Obviously I was getting the runaround. How soon would it be repaired? I asked. The man I had reached was embarrassed, I could tell, because he did not want to say flatly that cleaning streets in the black community was a pretty low priority. He would try to find out when the equipment would be repaired, he finally said, and he would call me back.

I remember joking about it to Dr. King, saying it didn't seem likely that the city was going to clean Auburn Avenue anytime soon. But I was wrong. The very next day we looked out and here came a large sweeper moving along Auburn. I don't think we saw much of that sweeper after that, but at least I got them to come that one day. Now I had more important things to worry about and didn't lose any sleep over sweepers cleaning up Auburn Avenue, but I think it is important to remember how much black and white affected everything then, even whether your streets got cleaned regularly.

I also remember settling in our rented apartment when we first moved to Atlanta. Our furniture was being shipped from Los Angeles, and I hurried around in those first days trying to get everything in order before it arrived. I got everything taken care of, but when I had the utilities turned on, I was a little surprised to be asked for a deposit. My previous experience had been, when we moved from Chicago to Los Angeles, that a deposit was not required if you had had previous service and had paid your bills. The deposit wasn't enormous, and I gave it hardly a thought at first, until I engaged in conversation with a white staffer at the SCLC who had moved to Atlanta about the time we did, whose situation was almost exactly the same as ours, and who had *not* been asked to make a deposit. The only reason I could see for the distinction was that we lived in a black neighborhood and the white staffer had moved into a mostly white one.

I decided to test this theory and I picked out two addresses, one in largely white northeast Atlanta and one in southwest Atlanta, a predominantly black neighborhood. I even tried to sound more black when I called and asked for one utility service for the southwest address, more white when I called about service for the other address. Sure enough, even though I described my circumstances in almost exactly the same words with each call, I was asked for a deposit on the account at the address in the black neighborhood but not for the account in the white neighborhood.

I made a point of getting the name of the woman who had asked for the deposit, and I headed for her office as soon as I got off the telephone. Once I got there, I really had to insist before I was permitted to speak to her. But she was quite apologetic when I told her exactly what I had done, and she offered to return my deposit. That part was fine, I said, even though the deposit was not a great deal of money. What was really wrong, I told her, was that the company would have a policy discriminating against the black community. I don't know if she agreed with me completely, but at least she seemed sorry.

Now, I don't know if this particular discriminatory policy changed in part because of my complaint, nor how soon afterward it changed, but it *did* change. However, I think it is especially important for younger people to understand the segregation patterns which only a few years ago affected almost every aspect of society.

The restaurant scene provides another example. Today, most Atlanta restaurants serve black and white patrons with the same courtesy, paying little attention to the number of blacks and whites present at any given time. Of course, this is a matter of law now, as well as of changing customs, but when I first came to Atlanta in the 1960s it seemed a huge breakthrough when the Magnolia Room at Rich's department store opened up and began serving black patrons. Macy's had a comfortable restaurant, too, and it soon followed suit. Again, it may be hard for younger people to understand the magnitude of these changes, or hard to imagine the world before these changes occurred.

I also remember from that time that black people were not free to browse through a store, that they often found store detectives following them. They simply assumed that any black person was a possible shoplifter. It was even worse if you carried a large purse, which I often did, because that was practically considered evidence that you were about to steal something. But I shouldn't imply that this was the case only in Atlanta. Once I was shopping in a very exclusive store in Los Angeles, and my companion noticed that this same man seemed to show up in every part of the store that we did. She confronted him finally and demanded to know why he was following us. Sure enough, he was a store detective, and he explained that I looked like a black woman who was a known shoplifter in expensive stores over the country, from New York to Los Angeles. I actually saw the woman somewhere later; someone pointed her out to me. She was taller than I am and her skin was a different shade. I didn't think she and I looked much alike, but I suppose the white detective thought *we all looked alike.* In that case my friend was a wealthy woman with a charge account at this expensive store, so she went straight to the manager and demanded an apology.

Back in Atlanta, a white friend of mine who worked at one of the leading department stores came to me one day exceedingly angry. She told me that she had just come from a meeting of all the salespeople in the store where the sales manager instructed them to carefully scrutinize all black customers; they were to note what black customers were wearing and any other details that would help them give good descriptions if any shoplifting occurred. What angered my friend was that they were not told to look for just *any* suspicious behavior, but specifically to observe the black customers.

"Blacks are seen as shoplifters, as unclean, as disreputable poor," Dr. Joe Feagin, who is white, wrote in the February, 1991, issue of the *American Sociological Review.* "No matter how affluent and influential, a black person cannot escape the stigma of being black even while relaxing and shopping," continued Feagin, a professor of sociology at the University of Florida.

This perception is rooted, in part, in statistics that show that a disproportionate number of blacks are below the poverty level or are charged with crimes and incarcerated. But the numbers do not reflect the growing number of blacks with disposable incomes and an inclination to spend. According to the Census Bureau, in 1989 (the latest year for which figures are available) there were almost a half-million black American households with incomes of $50,000 and up. While other racial and ethnic groups—and women—are also targets of discrimination in public places, blacks feel the brunt of such treatment because color immediately sets them apart.

. . .

When the treatment of individuals is based solely and strictly on the color of their skin, horrible experiences can result. One such experience happened to my sister Little; she was treated in a way that was not only grossly unfair, but that literally could have endangered her life.

The incident took place in Louisville, in May 1960, while we were attending the Kentucky Derby. Now, let me say that while this is the second unfortunate racial incident I have recounted as occurring in Louisville, the timing and location were coincidence. I have good friends in Louisville, and it was back then and is today a splendid community in many ways. My father-in-law was on the Louisville city council, and he dearly loved that city and its people. So I want to make plain that the incident I now describe could certainly have occurred in another city.

But it did occur in Louisville at the Kentucky Derby. My husband Ed and I, along with my sister and another friend, a black attorney from Chicago named Robert Tucker, were visiting purely for fun and planning to watch the Derby races.

As I explained earlier, my sister developed multiple sclerosis while still a young woman, and she had already contracted the disease by this time. She felt well enough to go with all of us to see the Derby that day, but it was a little cool, not cold enough really to bother the rest of us but cool enough so that she soon felt a chill. She held on valiantly for a time, not wanting to spoil our outing, but she clearly was feeling weak and more and more uncomfortable. Mr. Tucker offered to take her home, insisting that the rest of us stay and enjoy the Derby. Little really was feeling weak by the time they left the racetrack; Mr. Tucker was supporting her and finally picked her up and carried her. Fortunately, he was a tall, strong man, and my sister is not especially heavy.

Anyway, Mr. Tucker and my sister got to the edge of the parking area, and they could see their car down one row, not too far away. However, the traffic policeman there was directing people down to the end of the block and around to a certain entrance, which normally wouldn't have been a problem but which was in this case, because of my sister's illness and weakened condition. Mr. Tucker tried to explain to the white police officer, but he refused to listen and immediately arrested both of them for being drunk. Now, I don't happen to drink anything alcoholic, but my sister does, and so did my husband Ed and many of our friends. However, none of us had had anything to drink before going to the Derby, since we were planning to eat and drink afterward.

The rest of our party stayed through the races and then returned home, and we were upset to find neither my sister nor our friend Mr. Tucker there. I should add that not only had Mr. Tucker not had anything to drink, but he was also a member of a prestigious Chicago law firm — Moore, Ming & Leighton; yet he could get no one at the police station to listen to him. The only telephone number he knew to call in Louisville was that of my father-in-law's house, and we were all at the Derby.

Luckily, a black person at the Derby had witnessed the arrest and kept trying to call us and finally reached us when we got home. We then hurried down to rescue Little and Mr. Tucker, but my sister was so weakened by this time that she had to go to the hospital for an examination. The fact of it is that she was ill that day. Neither she nor Mr. Tucker had had anything alcoholic to drink. But because they were black, they were arrested and thrown into jail like just another couple of "drunk niggers."

•   •   •

I remember another incident as recently as the 1980s, when disco dancing became popular in Atlanta. A white man who worked at a disco called me to say that he was distressed because they had a quota on how many black men could enter the establishment at night. The management frankly did not want too many black men dancing with white women. It worked this way. A lot of women, black and white, would go to the place, and they were admitted. And if a black couple arrived, they too were admitted. But the employees were instructed to limit the number of single black men and, when they reached the designated number, to refuse any others, using all kinds of different excuses.

Some of these incidents are recent enough to indicate that Dr. King's dream of an end to racism still is a long way from being realized. Every time I get ready to say to myself, well, we have overcome, we have made the dream a reality, we have changed society so that it reflects our mixture and diversity and togetherness the way it should . . . just when I think I am ready to say all that, especially when people ask if I don't think we have made a lot of progress and are finally getting there, something will come up that makes me realize we still have such a long way to go.

Consider the recent police brutality in Los Angeles, my old home city, even in 1991 — white police officers standing around while other white police officers beat a black man half to death. I fear it could have happened in any number of other cities, and I know a great many people have seen the video tape and expressed concern and embarrassment, including President George Bush. It has struck me, however, that a number of white people I know, people I consider liberal and fairminded, are simply reluctant to talk about it. It troubles me. I don't know if this is a temporary aberration or not, but it is as if the kind of enlightened white people whom I knew in the 1960s, who were concerned and eager to talk about what was happening in the civil rights movement, are in 1991 skirting this issue of white police brutality against a black suspect in custody. I have observed this with acute interest, not sure yet what it means.

•   •   •

What would Dr. King be doing and saying if he were still alive today? I often wonder. I know he would be speaking out against cases of police brutality and the remnants of racism in our society, working hard to do a little more about the things he cared so deeply about. He was always concerned about poverty, and I know that today's poverty problem would just gnaw at him. He felt you were dealing with behavior when you were dealing with racism, behavior that could be changed, but people in poverty were suffering so directly. People do not willfully decide to be poor.

I think people do *decide* to practice discrimination. It is finally a matter of choice whether you are going to be fair-minded or bigoted. But poverty most often traps people without their ever having choices. You can walk through some streets and see people huddled on grates to keep warm, and I have seen long lines in Atlanta of people waiting hungrily to get a bowl of soup. I believe that if Dr. King were still alive he would just be working overtime to feed those hungry people.

There is no question that racial barriers still exist on many fronts, too. The problem of school segregation was supposedly solved by the U.S. Supreme Court decision in 1954, but we are still dealing with that in 1991. Housing was supposed to be desegregated after the passage of the Open Housing laws, but I saw an article just a few weeks ago about white people in Michigan, as far north as you can get in the United States without crossing into Canada, trying to prevent black people from buying houses in their expensive neighborhood. Again, this is in 1991. Economic development is a priority for minorities, and many try to start businesses with the help of whatever loans, but people tell me that it is more difficult to get such loans now than it was a few years ago.

There are other areas of concern.

• • •

The savings and loan industry has had its share of problems in recent months, but I have kept an article that appeared in the *Atlanta Journal-Constitution*, April 17, 1989, which reflects the deplorable condition of the industry long before their plight was made public. The article quoted a report released by the Institute for Southern Studies which said, "The leaders of the South's largest savings and loan associations are an exclusive club limited almost entirely to white men. . . . Race and sex . . . not income or ability . . . generally determine who makes policy decisions at savings and loans, who takes the good jobs, who gets loans."

Of the 1,270 directors of the ten largest savings and loans in the thirteen-state Southern region, all but twelve were white, the report stated. Nine were black and three were Hispanic. There were no minorities on the boards of directors of any of the ten largest savings and loans in North Carolina, Tennessee, Arkansas, Mississippi, West Virginia, and Kentucky. Five others (Georgia, Alabama, Texas, South Carolina, and Louisiana) had one each. Across the region, white men held 1,219 of the seats . . . women held forty-two seats.

Things have changed considerably now for the savings and loan industry. The bail-out participants are all colors, races, and creeds. Those who are called upon to save the industry are providing their tax money without regard to sex, color, creed or ethnic background.

• • •

It was twenty years ago (1971) that the Federal Communications Commission (FCC) responded to the women's movement by altering Equal Employment Opportunity rules to include females. That sent television stations and networks scurrying to hire women.

Though their number remains far too small, women now occupy important behind-the-scenes positions in newsrooms across the nation. Even female news directors have emerged along the way, and several women have become famous on-air personalities — among them Diane Sawyer, Connie Chung, Catherine Crier, Rebecca Chase, Deborah Norville, Lesley Stahl, Judy Woodruff, Mary Tillotson, and Rita Braver. The list is significantly smaller, however, for black women. That scant roll includes ABC's Carole Simpson, CNN's Lyn Vaughn, and PBS's Charlayne Hunter-Gault.

In the television industry, men and women climb different and unequal ladders, and a similar disparity exists between white and black women. While women in general are aiming to crash through the "glass ceiling," minority women still find themselves "stuck on the ground floor." Until these conditions become more equitable, we all need to keep marching toward the goals of parity and equality in the marketplace.

•   •   •

Race is still America's most pressing domestic issue. No wonder. There are more black males in our jails and prison cells than in the dormitories of our colleges and universities. The average black boy is more likely to go to prison than to college. His life expectancy is falling, and he is seven times more likely to be murdered than a white boy. The chances are almost two to one that he was brought up in a fatherless household. The statistics from Black America are staggering.

The *Economist*, in its March 30, 1991 issue, offers an overseas view on "Blacks in America." It summarizes its conclusions in this statement: "America is riding high on a wave of post Gulf confidence, but one part of the country is still missing out: the poverty-ridden ghettos where millions of black Americans live. George Bush cannot afford to ignore them." Sealed off in inner-city ghettos, bypassed by fly-over freeways, black America is suffering out of sight. The ghettos are a nation apart, and their young people are growing up physically and psychologically separated from the American mainstream.

Last year, the unemployment rate for black Americans was 10.5%, more than twice that of white Americans; approximately 43% of black children are born poor. The job market is bleak for many Americans; for black Americans the situation is critical. Jobs simply aren't there. Discussion of the issue elicits two opinions: the liberal thinker tends to stress that black people "cannot work." For many young black people, the only jobs that offer a secure future and a steady income are in the military. Conservatives tend to stress that black people "will not work." They say that, in spite of the recession, the newspapers are filled with want ads. That view is widespread. A recent poll by the National Opinion Research Center showed that 78% of whites think blacks are more likely than whites to "prefer to live off welfare." But whatever the reason, whether it is "cannot" or "will not," the fact remains . . . they don't have jobs.

The National Opinion Research Center released its survey in January, 1991, and the results were very distressing to those of us who are optimistic, who want to believe that progress in racial understanding has moved forward to the point that we are almost "there." The survey showed many white Americans still have negative attitudes toward blacks. The poll reflected these findings: 62.2% felt black Americans are less hard-working than whites. Nearly 54% felt black people are less intelligent than whites. The report points up the fact that while most whites support racial equality, they still cling to negative stereotypes about intelligence, violence, and patriotism among minorities.

•　　•　　•

The big thing that continues to hurt is the dehumanizing *feeling* of racism. You wonder all the time if you are going to be accepted, how you will be treated if you want to buy a house or a car, or whether an insurance company might redline your neighborhood. You think you are trying to be a good citizen, conforming to expectations by buying insurance to cover your house or your car, and you find you're paying a double price because you are black and live in a black neighborhood. That kind of discrimination seems inexplicable in 1991.

And racism now takes so many subtle forms. It is no longer as overt as being refused service in a restaurant or not being allowed to try on clothes in a store, but it is still real.

Here is a good example. Suppose you are waiting your turn at the perfume counter in a store and you are standing patiently behind one customer, knowing that you should be next to be served. But then a white customer walks up as the salesperson is finishing with the one customer ahead of you, and, instead of turning to you though clearly aware that you have been standing there waiting, she turns instead to the new white customer. Now is that racism? You can't really make such a charge because it is not absolutely clear, but that is what you suspect. You think—indeed, you know—that the salesperson overlooked you deliberately when all you wanted was to be treated with fairness. That happened to me recently. After a while you put such occurrences in a category, knowing that there are people still who will avoid you or snub you if they can, and as often as they can.

I spoke to a group of female executives in suburban Atlanta not long ago, and I thought later that part of my "sermon" always comes out the same, that we all have to come up with ways to live together, that each of us must be imbued with the spirit of doing what we can where we can. Do what you can wherever you are. No matter what kind of speech I am making, whatever the subject, I always get back to that theme. Prejudice is so self-limiting. Prejudice means the individual fails to grow, fails to be enlarged by encounters and experiences and exchanges with others, fails to learn and appreciate the diversity of human kind. What person who aspires to be intelligent and modern and spiritually alive could want to practice discrimination and segregation? No fairminded person does.

People's consciences are pricked, I find, when I deliver this "sermon." Some feel guilt, I suppose, and often say to me that they know they have practiced discrimination in certain ways but they want to try to do what they can to make things better. Their responses are often so sincere that I believe many follow through and try to help change things. I use the word "sermon" because I know that the responses I get may be like what happens in a real church. We hear a good sermon from the minister and sit there nodding and thinking how we are going to live sin-free lives, but we leave church and walk right back into sin again. Maybe I am overly optimistic when I describe the response I get, but even if I have touched only a few people and if they touch others, then perhaps after a while everybody will capture the spirit and we will overcome the barrier of racial prejudice. We are all the same under the skin, as Dr. King so often said.

What hurts a white person will more than likely hurt me. During the war in the Persian Gulf I don't think anyone asked his neighbor on the firing line about the color of his skin. More likely the question was, can you shoot straight? Our military people in the Persian Gulf all had the same mission and won that war brilliantly, but until all of us in this country have the same sense of mission to dispel prejudice we will not win the war on the home front. When enough Americans perceive that racism and prejudice are *also* the enemy, then we can win that war, too.

The black Americans who fought in the Persian Gulf are as proud of their victory as anyone. But what happens when they come back home to reality? Will they still face assorted discriminations on other fronts? Throughout history black Americans have fought valiantly in all our wars, often hoping their participation would mean equality and freedom, and then they have come back home to slavery and segregation and discrimination. They have proven they will fight for their country, but what happens when the battles are over? People say they are so proud of all of our military people in the wake of the victory in the Persian Gulf. But being proud for an instant in time is not enough.

At some point, human beings will come to realize that there is no victory in separation—no victory in racial or sexual discrimination.

From a practical standpoint I tend to believe that people of good will, the decision-makers and political leaders and spiritual leaders, will come to understand that a country with our vast resources—material, intellectual, and spiritual—simply cannot be permitted to disintegrate because of prejudice. On those pragmatic grounds, if nothing more, I have to believe that we are becoming steadily more civilized and more human. I also believe that we are going to have a spiritual rebirth in our nation, including the realization that the old prejudiced way of treating human beings was wrong and did not produce desirable results. There must be a new and better and improved way.

We must do all we can, black and white together, to change negative attitudes wherever they exist and lift the veil of ignorance so that all people can rid themselves of that "certain blindness" noted in my husband's book, so that all can live and enjoy the richness of a free and just society.

Challenges remain, especially the great, pressing challenge to encourage people of good will to work together to overcome prejudice and poverty and cruelty.

I am still marching, Martin. I will keep marching until we achieve justice and equality for all people.

INDEX